hamlyn cookery club

Winter
warmers

hamlyn cookery club
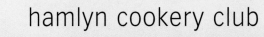

Winter
warmers

First published in 2000 by Hamlyn
an imprint of Octopus Publishing Group Ltd
2–4 Heron Quays
London E14 4JP

British Library Cataloguing-in-Publication Data
A catalogue record for this book is available from the
British Library.

ISBN 0 600 60072 6

Printed in China

Copy Editor: Heather Thomas
Creative Director: Keith Martin
Design Manager: Bryan Dunn
Designer: Ginny Zeal
Jacket Photography: Sean Myers
Picture Researcher: Rosie Garai
Production Controller: Lisa Moore

Notes

1 Both metric and imperial measurements have been given in all recipes. Use one set of measurements only and not a mixture of both.

2 Standard level spoon measurements are used in all recipes.
1 tablespoon = one 15 ml spoon
1 teaspoon = one 5 ml spoon

3 Eggs should be medium unless otherwise stated. The Department of Health advises that eggs should not be consumed raw. This book may contain dishes made with raw or lightly cooked eggs. It is prudent for more vulnerable people such as pregnant or nursing mothers, the elderly, babies and young children to avoid these dishes. Once prepared, these dishes should be refrigerated and eaten promptly.

4 Milk should be full fat unless otherwise stated.

5 Fresh herbs should be used unless otherwise stated. If unavailable use dried herbs as an alternative but halve the quantities stated.

6 Pepper should be freshly ground black pepper unless otherwise stated.

7 Ovens should be preheated to the specified temperature – if using a fan-assisted oven, follow the manufacturer's instructions for adjusting the time and temperature.

8 Measurements for canned food have been given as a standard metric equivalent.

Contents

Introduction

When the weather is cold and there's a gale blowing outside, you can cheer yourself up with some warming food. Hot stews, classic casseroles, spicy exotic dishes and comforting puddings will all help keep out the winter chill. Winter food is often more substantial than summer food, however, this doesn't mean eating heavy, stodgy food. *Winter Warmers* is a celebration of healthy seasonal ingredients (poultry, game, meat, root vegetables, cabbage and sprouts) which are used in nourishing dishes.

SEASONINGS AND FLAVOURINGS

Stews and casseroles offer a comforting mixture of flavours and these can be enhanced by using different herbs, spices and flavourings. Experiment to find the right combinations and balance. Here are some tips to help you:
• Try adding some thinly pared orange peel to a beef casserole for a rich aromatic sauce.
• Sage, prunes, sliced apple and orange juice all complement pork.
• You can create a delicious North African-style tagine by adding dried fruit, such as prunes and apricots, to a lamb stew or casserole. Flavour with saffron and ground spices.
• If you have the time, making your own meat, chicken, fish or vegetable stock is well worth the effort and will enhance the flavour of the finished dish.
• Make a rich sauce for a game, meat or chicken casserole by adding some full-bodied red wine, Madeira or port.

MAKING STOCK

Nothing could be easier than making a flavoursome stock, and it will taste so much better than commercially made stock cubes and powders. Here is a quick guide to making the basic stocks.
• **Beef stock**
Put some beef or veal bones in a large pan with a halved onion, a chopped carrot, leek and celery stick, bay leaf and sprig of parsley. Add a little salt and some peppercorns and cover with water. Boil gently for 3 hours, then strain and cool. Keep for up to 3 days in the refrigerator or freeze.

• Chicken stock

Put a chicken carcass in a deep pan with the same ingredients as beef stock, except the veal or beef bones. Bring to the boil, skim off any scum, then cover and simmer for 3 hours. Cool, strain and refrigerate for up to 3 days. This stock freezes well.

• Fish stock

Place fish trimmings, 2 roughly chopped carrots, 1 onion, 2 celery sticks and 2 leeks in a large pan with 2 bay leaves, 4 parsley sprigs, 4 thyme sprigs, 6 white peppercorns and 1 teaspoon of sea salt. Cover with 900 ml (1½ pints) cold water and 900 ml (1½ pints) dry white wine. Bring to the boil, skim the surface to remove any scum, cover and simmer for 30 minutes. Strain through a sieve, return to the pan and simmer, uncovered, until the stock is reduced to about 900 ml (1½ pints). Cool and refrigerate.

• Vegetable stock

Place a chopped onion, leek, 2 carrots and 2 celery sticks in a large pan with 2 chopped tomatoes, 2 sprigs of parsley and a good pinch of salt. Cover with 1.2 litres (2 pints) cold water and bring to the boil. Simmer for 2 hours, then strain, cool and refrigerate for up to 3 days or freeze.

THICKENING STEWS AND CASSEROLES

You don't necessarily have to thicken a stew or casserole – many cook down to a rich coating sauce. However, flour can be added by coating the meat in seasoned flour before cooking; or by adding a little beurre manié (softened butter mixed with flour to a paste) at the end. Just drop small pieces into the sauce and cook, stirring, until the sauce thickens.

COOKING AHEAD

The wonderful thing about casseroles is that you can make them in advance and then leave them to cook slowly in a low oven. A casserole made in advance can be reheated the following day and the combination of slow cooking and resting overnight improves the flavour. If you're making a casserole a day ahead, cool it thoroughly before refrigerating it, then gently reheat in a preheated oven, 180°C (350°F), Gas Mark 4, for 30–40 minutes until piping hot.

Stews and casseroles freeze well so it's a good idea to double up and make twice as much as you need. You can then freeze half the quantity in a covered foil or sealed plastic container. Allow to defrost thoroughly before reheating.

Everyday Dishes

125 ml (4 fl oz) dry red wine
1 tablespoon tomato purée
2 tablespoons cornflour
50 ml (2 fl oz) red wine
salt and pepper

Soak the mushrooms in the warm water for 30 minutes. Drain the mushrooms, reserving the soaking liquid. Chop the mushrooms roughly and then set aside. Strain and retain the liquid.

Heat the oil in a large flameproof casserole and cook the chicken, skin-side down, for 10 minutes, turning occasionally, until browned. Remove and set aside.

Add the leeks and onion to the casserole and cook for 5 minutes, stirring occasionally. Add the ham, garlic, marjoram, rosemary, thyme and savory. Cook for 1 minute. Stir in the reserved mushrooms and soaking liquid, the stock, red wine and tomato purée and season with salt and pepper.

Return the chicken pieces to the casserole. Cover and cook over a medium to low heat for 25 minutes. Remove the breast pieces from the casserole and keep them warm on a heated serving platter. Continue cooking the dark meat pieces for another 10 minutes, then remove and transfer to the serving platter.

Skim the fat off the sauce and then bring to the boil. Combine the cornflour and red wine in a cup

Braised Italian Hunter's Chicken

25 g (1 oz) dried Italian (porcini)
  mushrooms
350 ml (12 fl oz) warm water
50 ml (2 fl oz) olive oil
2 x 1.5 kg (3 lb) chickens, each cut
  into 8 serving pieces

2 leeks, white part only, sliced
1 large onion, chopped
75 g (3 oz) unsmoked ham, cubed
2 garlic cloves, finely chopped
1 tablespoon marjoram, finely
  chopped
1 tablespoon rosemary, finely
  chopped
¾ teaspoon thyme
½ teaspoon savory, finely chopped
400 ml (14 fl oz) chicken stock

until smooth. Using a whisk, blend the cornflour mixture into the sauce and simmer for 2–3 minutes until thick and smooth. To serve, pour the sauce over the chicken pieces.

Serves 8

Chicken and Sausage Casserole with Dumplings

3 x 425 g (14 oz) cans tomatoes

2 teaspoons sugar

1 x 1.25 kg (2½ lb) chicken, cut into
   8 pieces

1 tablespoon olive oil

500 g (1 lb) uncooked Italian
   sausages, pricked

1 large onion, chopped

125 g (4 oz) button mushrooms, sliced

1 green pepper, cored, deseeded and
   cubed

1 garlic clove, finely chopped

125 ml (4 fl oz) chicken stock

125 ml (4 fl oz) dry white wine

2 tablespoons oregano, finely
   chopped

salt and pepper

Dumplings:

50 g (2 oz) self-raising flour

50 g (2 oz) soft white breadcrumbs

2 tablespoons shredded suet

1 tablespoon parsley, finely chopped

2 teaspoons lemon rind, finely grated

1 egg, beaten

Cook the tomatoes over a medium heat for 20 minutes, stirring them occasionally, until they are reduced to 475 ml (16 fl oz). Stir in the sugar and then set aside.

Season the chicken pieces with salt and pepper. Heat the oil in a large flameproof casserole, and add the chicken, skin-side down, and the sausages. Cook for 10 minutes, turning frequently, until brown. Drain off the excess fat and discard.

Add the cooked tomatoes, onion, mushrooms, green pepper, garlic, stock, wine, oregano and season with salt and pepper. Stir well and then bring to the boil. Remove from the heat, cover the casserole and cook in a preheated oven, 200°C (400°F), Gas Mark 6, for about 25 minutes.

Meanwhile, make the dumplings. Mix together the flour, breadcrumbs, suet, parsley, lemon rind and season with salt and pepper. Make a well in the centre of the mixture and then place the egg in the well. Drawing in the flour mixture from the sides, quickly combine the ingredients to make a soft dough. With floured hands, shape the dumpling mixture into 8 equal-sized balls.

Place the dumpling balls in the casserole. Cover and continue cooking in the preheated oven for a further 20 minutes or until the dumplings are cooked. Serve the casserole hot with boiled carrots and a selection of green vegetables.

Serves 4

left: braised Italian hunter's chicken
above: *chicken and sausage casserole with dumplings*

Somerset Chicken

4 tablespoons plain flour
4 boneless, skinless chicken breasts,
    about 150 g (5 oz) each, cut into
    bite-sized pieces
1 onion, finely chopped
175 g (6 oz) button mushrooms,
    sliced
2 tablespoons parsley, finely chopped
2 teaspoons mixed dried herbs
1 kg (2 lb) potatoes, thinly sliced
300 ml (½ pint) chicken stock
300 ml (½ pint) dry cider
salt and pepper
chopped parsley, to garnish

Put the flour in a plastic bag and
season with salt and pepper. Add
the chicken pieces and tightly seal
the opening of the bag. Shake well
to coat the chicken thoroughly.
Transfer the chicken pieces to a
large casserole with the onion,
mushrooms, parsley, herbs and
season with salt and pepper.

Arrange the potatoes on the top
of the casserole. Pour in the chicken
stock and cider. The potatoes should
just be covered with liquid. Cover
the casserole and then cook in a
preheated oven, 190°C (375°F), Gas
Mark 5, for 1 hour.

Take the lid off the casserole and
continue cooking for 15 minutes
until the top is brown. Garnish with
the chopped parsley and serve.

Serves 4

Braised Chicken with New Potatoes and Paprika

Sweet Hungarian paprika, for which
there is no real substitute, is available in
delicatessens and supermarkets.

2 tablespoons vegetable oil
200 g (7 oz) rashers of streaky bacon,
    rinded and cut into strips
1 x 1.5 kg (3 lb) chicken, cut into
    8 pieces
1 large onion, chopped
1 large green pepper, cored,
    deseeded and chopped
1 garlic clove, finely chopped
4 tablespoons plain flour
2 tablespoons sweet Hungarian
    paprika
600 ml (1 pint) chicken stock
125 ml (4 fl oz) dry white wine
12 small red or white new potatoes,
    halved
300 ml (½ pint) soured cream
salt and pepper

Heat the oil in a large flameproof
casserole, add the bacon and cook
for 5 minutes, stirring frequently.
Remove the bacon and set aside.
Pour off all but 3 tablespoons of fat.

Season the chicken pieces with
salt and pepper. Place them in the
casserole, skin-side down, over a
medium-high heat. Brown, turning
occasionally, for 10–15 minutes.
Remove the chicken and set aside.

Add the onion to the casserole
and cook, stirring occasionally, for
5 minutes. Add the green pepper
and garlic and cook for 1 minute.
Blend in 2 tablespoons of the flour
and the paprika and cook for 2
minutes, stirring constantly. Using
a whisk, gradually blend in the
stock and wine. Bring to the boil
and cook until the sauce is smooth
and thick.

Return the chicken and bacon to
the sauce. Arrange the potatoes
around the chicken. Cover and cook
over a medium-low heat for about
30 minutes. Remove the breast
pieces from the casserole and keep
warm on a heated serving platter.
Continue cooking the dark meat
pieces for another 10 minutes.

Remove the remaining chicken pieces and keep warm. Test the potatoes; if they are not tender, cover the casserole and cook over a medium-low heat until they are cooked. Remove with a slotted spoon and arrange them around the chicken pieces.

To finish the sauce, turn down the heat to very low. Combine the soured cream and remaining flour in a small bowl until smooth. Using a whisk, stir into the sauce. Cook gently for 2 minutes. Pour the sauce over the chicken and potatoes. Serve immediately with tagliatelle and a green vegetable.

Serves 4–6

left: braised chicken with new potatoes and paprika
below: turkey hash

Turkey Hash

40 g (1½ oz) butter
1 onion, finely chopped
1 red pepper, cored, deseeded and diced
250 g (8 oz) button mushrooms, thinly sliced
1 garlic clove, finely chopped
500 g (1 lb) cooked turkey meat, cubed
300 g (10 oz) turkey stuffing, cubed
300 ml (½ pint) double or whipping cream
250 ml (8 fl oz) turkey or chicken stock
125 ml (4 fl oz) turkey gravy
2 tablespoons cornflour
15 g (½ oz) parsley, finely chopped
⅛ teaspoon ground nutmeg
25 g (1 oz) Gruyère cheese, grated
salt and pepper

Melt the butter in a flameproof casserole over a moderate heat. Add the onion and then cook, stirring frequently, for 5 minutes. Add the red pepper, mushrooms and garlic and cook for 3 minutes until the mushrooms begin to soften. Add the turkey and stuffing, then cook for 5 minutes, stirring occasionally. Remove the casserole from the heat and set aside.

In a saucepan, combine the cream with 175 ml (6 fl oz) of the stock and the gravy. Bring to the boil. Blend the cornflour and the remaining stock in a cup until smooth and, using a whisk, stir into the sauce. Simmer for 2–3 minutes, stirring constantly, until smooth and thick. Remove from the heat and add the parsley, nutmeg, and season with salt and pepper to taste.

Pour the sauce into the casserole and sprinkle with cheese. Cover and cook in a preheated oven, 180°C (350°F), Gas Mark 4, for 25 minutes until heated through. Serve with bread and a fresh salad.

Serves 6

French Café Beef Casserole

25 ml (1 fl oz) vegetable oil

750 g (1½ lb) chuck steak, trimmed and cut into 2.5 cm (1 inch) cubes

1 large onion, thinly sliced

175 g (6 oz) button mushrooms, quartered

4 rashers of streaky bacon, rinded and chopped

250 g (8 oz) can tomatoes

175 ml (6 fl oz) beef stock

2 garlic cloves, finely chopped

1 teaspoon allspice

½ teaspoon dried mixed herbs

2 tablespoons plain flour

75 ml (3 fl oz) dry red wine

50 g (2 oz) butter, softened

1 tablespoon wholegrain mustard

8 slices of French bread, cut diagonally in 1 cm (½ inch) slices

salt and pepper

sprigs of parsley, to garnish

Heat the oil in a large flameproof casserole, then add the meat and brown for 5–10 minutes, stirring frequently. Remove the meat from the casserole with a slotted spoon and set aside.

Add the onion, mushrooms and bacon to the casserole, and cook for 10 minutes until the onion is tender and the bacon is crisp. Drain off the excess fat and discard.

Return the meat to the casserole and blend in the tomatoes, stock, garlic, allspice and mixed herbs and season with salt and pepper.

Combine the flour and red wine in a cup until smooth and stir into the casserole. Cover and cook in a preheated oven, 150°C (300°F), Gas Mark 2, for 2 hours until the meat is cooked and tender.

To finish, combine the butter with the mustard. Spread the mixture evenly on one side of each bread slice. Arrange the bread slices, overlapping and mustard-side up, on top of the casserole. Brown under a preheated hot grill. Garnish with the parsley sprigs and serve immediately.

Serves 4–6

above: French café beef casserole

Chicken and Broccoli Roll-ups

65 g (2½ oz) butter

6 x 150 g (5 oz) boneless, skinless
  chicken thighs

6 small broccoli florets

250 ml (8 fl oz) boiling water

125 ml (4 fl oz) chicken stock

2 small onions, thinly sliced

2 tablespoons plain flour

½ tablespoon basil, finely chopped

¼ teaspoon celery salt

125 ml (4 fl oz) milk

6 x 25 g (1 oz) slices Swiss
  cheese

salt and pepper

Melt 2 tablespoons of the butter in
a large frying pan, add the chicken
thighs and brown for 10 minutes,
turning them frequently. Remove
the chicken thighs and set aside.

Dip the broccoli florets in the
boiling water for a few seconds,
then remove and dip them into the
chicken stock. Discard the water
or reserve for another use. Sprinkle
the broccoli with salt and then set
aside. Reserve the chicken stock.

Cook the onions in 2 tablespoons
of the butter for 5–10 minutes,
stirring frequently, until tender.
Sprinkle the onions with the flour,
basil and celery salt and season with
salt and pepper. Cook for a further
2–3 minutes, stirring constantly.

Using a whisk, gradually stir in
the reserved chicken stock and the
milk. Cook gently for 5 minutes,
stirring constantly, until smooth
and thickened. Set aside.

To assemble each roll-up, wrap
1 slice of the cheese around 1
broccoli floret. Wrap 1 chicken
thigh around the cheese and
broccoli. Secure with a wooden
cocktail stick or a small metal
skewer. Season each roll-up lightly
with salt and pepper.

Grease a casserole dish with the
remaining butter, then arrange the
roll-ups in the casserole and pour
the sauce over them. Cover the
casserole and cook in a preheated
oven, 180°C (350°F), Gas Mark 4,
for 20 minutes.

Uncover the casserole and then
continue cooking for 20 minutes.
Serve immediately with creamed
potatoes and a tomato salad.

Serves 6

Main Meal Minestrone

2 tablespoons olive oil

2 onions, chopped

4 rashers of streaky bacon, rinded and
  diced

175 g (6 oz) tomatoes, skinned and
  chopped

175 g (6 oz) haricot beans, soaked
  overnight

1.8 litres (3 pints) water

1 teaspoon dried basil

2 carrots, diced

2 celery sticks, chopped

250 g (8 oz) cabbage, shredded

salt and pepper

Meatballs:

500 g (1 lb) lean minced beef

2 tablespoons fresh white
  breadcrumbs

1 small onion, finely chopped

1 teaspoon dried thyme

1 egg, beaten

To serve:

1 tablespoon tomato purée

2 tablespoons Parmesan, finely grated
  cheese, plus extra to serve

Heat the oil in a deep flameproof
casserole. Add the onions and
bacon and fry for 2–3 minutes. Add
the tomatoes and drained haricot
beans and cover with water. Stir in
the basil and then season with salt
and pepper.

Cover with a lid or foil and cook
in a preheated oven, 160°C (325°F),
Gas Mark 3, for 2 hours.

Meanwhile, make the meatballs.
Mix together all the ingredients
until well blended and season with
salt and pepper. Use floured hands
to mould the mixture into about 50
tiny meatballs.

Add the carrots, celery, cabbage
and meatballs to the casserole and
cook for a further 30 minutes or
until the vegetables are tender and
the meatballs are cooked through.

Stir in the tomato purée and
2 tablespoons of grated Parmesan.
Season to taste with salt and pepper.
Serve with extra Parmesan and
crusty French bread.

Serves 6

Piquant Beef Short Ribs

2 tablespoons vegetable oil
1.5 kg (3 lb) beef short ribs or pork spareribs, cut into serving pieces
1 onion, finely chopped
375 ml (13 fl oz) tomato ketchup
250 ml (8 fl oz) water
50 ml (2 fl oz) red wine vinegar
1 garlic clove, finely chopped
3 tablespoons Worcestershire sauce
2 tablespoons sugar
1 tablespoon Dijon mustard
salt

Heat the oil in a large flameproof casserole over a medium heat. Add the ribs and onion and cook for 10 minutes until browned all over.

Gently combine all the remaining ingredients in a bowl and pour over the ribs, stirring well to coat. Cover the casserole and then cook in a preheated oven, 180°C (350°F), Gas Mark 4, for 2 hours until tender.

Skim off the excess fat and serve the casserole immediately with some baked potatoes and coleslaw.

Serves 4–5

Chicken in a Tureen

1 celery heart
1 x 2 kg (4 lb) chicken, tied and wing tips removed
1.8 litres (3 pints) chicken stock
1.8 litres (3 pints) water
4 young carrots, peeled
4 small onions, peeled
4 small turnips, trimmed
4 small leeks, white part only and tied in a bundle
12 sprigs of parsley
1 sprig of thyme
1 bay leaf
50 g (2 oz) butter, softened
50 g (2 oz) plain flour
salt and pepper
2 tablespoons parsley, finely chopped, to garnish

Stuff the celery inside the chicken and place in a large flameproof casserole. Cover with the stock and water. Bring to the boil, removing the scum when necessary. Cover and simmer for 15 minutes.

Reduce the heat and add the carrots, onions, turnips and leeks. Tie the parsley, thyme and bay leaf in a piece of muslin to make a bouquet garni. Place in the casserole and season with salt and pepper. Cover and simmer for 1 hour.

Discard the bouquet garni and transfer the chicken and vegetables to a heated serving platter. Remove the string and discard.

Strain off 900 ml (1½ pints) of the cooking liquid into a pan and bring to the boil. Combine the butter and flour to make a thick paste. While stirring, drop small pieces of the paste into the boiling liquid. Cook for 5 minutes until the sauce is smooth and thick. Adjust the seasoning to taste, if necessary, and then transfer to a sauceboat.

Carve the chicken into pieces and serve garnished with the chopped parsley. Hand the sauce separately.

Serves 4–6

Stewed Chicken with Spring Vegetables

75 g (3 oz) butter
3 tablespoons vegetable oil
1 x 2 kg (4 lb) chicken, cut into
  8 pieces
1 carrot, finely chopped
1 large onion, finely chopped
1 celery stick, finely chopped
900 ml (1½ pints) chicken stock
250 ml (8 fl oz) dry white wine
12 small onions, peeled
6 small carrots, cut into short
  lengths
6 small turnips, cubed
6 small new potatoes, halved
3 tablespoons chervil, finely chopped
2 tablespoons basil, finely chopped
1 tablespoon thyme leaves
1 teaspoon tarragon, finely chopped
1 bay leaf
250 g (8 oz) broccoli florets
125 g (4 oz) frozen peas, thawed, or
  cooked fresh peas
3 egg yolks
125 ml (4 fl oz) double cream
salt and pepper

Heat 3 tablespoons of the butter together with the oil in a large frying pan. Add the chicken pieces, skin-side down, and cook them for 10 minutes, turning occasionally, until brown all over. Remove the chicken from the pan and place in a large flameproof casserole.

Pour off all but 3 tablespoons of the fat from the frying pan. Add the chopped carrot, onion and celery. Reduce the heat and then cook for 10 minutes, stirring frequently. Add 250 ml (8 fl oz) of the stock and bring to the boil. Boil, scraping the bottom of the pan to incorporate all the bits, for 3 minutes. Pour the mixture over the chicken pieces.

Add the remaining stock and wine to the casserole. Bring to the boil and then simmer, partially covered, for 1½ hours, removing the scum occasionally.

Melt the remaining butter in a large frying pan and add the small onions, carrot lengths, turnips and potatoes. Cook, stirring frequently, for 10 minutes until lightly browned.

Transfer the mixture with a slotted spoon to the casserole. Add all the herbs and cook gently for 15–25 minutes until the chicken and vegetables are tender. Add the broccoli and peas and cook for a further 4–5 minutes until tender.

Remove the chicken and the vegetables to a heated deep platter with a slotted spoon. Keep warm.

Skim the fat off the casserole and discard the bay leaf. Add salt and pepper to taste. Using a whisk, thoroughly combine the egg yolks and cream in a bowl. Whisk in 125 ml (4 fl oz) of the hot cooking liquid. Slowly stir the egg mixture into the casserole and cook over a very low heat for 3 minutes, stirring constantly, until thickened. Do not boil or the sauce may curdle. Pour the sauce over the chicken and serve with warm French bread, if liked.

Serves 8

left: piquant beef short ribs
above: stewed chicken with spring vegetables

Beef Rouladen

These are a German speciality. The piquancy of the mustard and dill pickles is a good counterpoint to the relative blandness of the meat. Make sure that the beef slices are pounded very thinly by your butcher, otherwise they will be difficult to roll up neatly.

6 x 150 g (5 oz) slices of topside or
   silverside of beef
1 tablespoon Dijon mustard
1 onion, finely chopped
1½ dill pickles, cut lengthways into
   quarters
1 tablespoon vegetable oil
15 g (½ oz) butter
125 g (4 oz) button mushrooms,
   sliced
450 ml (¾ pint) beef stock
125 ml (4 fl oz) dry white wine
1½ tablespoons cornflour
salt and pepper

2 tablespoons parsley, finely chopped,
   to garnish

Spread the beef slices evenly with the mustard. Season with salt and pepper and sprinkle the onion over each slice. Top with a dill pickle quarter, then roll up and secure with wooden cocktail sticks.

Heat the oil and butter in a large flameproof casserole set over a moderate heat. Add the beef rouladen and, turning frequently, brown on all sides for 10 minutes. Add the mushrooms together with 350 ml (12 fl oz) stock and the wine.

Cover the casserole and bake in a preheated oven, 180°C (350°F), Gas Mark 4, for about 1¼ hours.

Transfer the rouladen to a heated serving platter and keep warm. Bring the sauce to the boil over a high heat. Combine the cornflour and remaining stock in a cup until smooth. Using a whisk, blend the

cornflour mixture into the sauce. Cook for 2–3 minutes until the sauce is smooth and has thickened.

To serve, pour the sauce over the rouladen and then sprinkle with the parsley. Serve with boiled potatoes, red cabbage and cucumber and a dish of soured cream.

Serves 6

Veal Ragoût

2 tablespoons vegetable oil
1 kg (2 lb) stewing veal, cubed
3 tablespoons plain flour
1 garlic clove, finely chopped
900 ml (1½ pints) chicken stock
2 tablespoons tomato purée
1 tablespoon finely chopped parsley
1 tablespoon thyme leaves
1 bay leaf, crushed
40 g (1½ oz) butter

3 onions, quartered

4 carrots, cut into 2.5 cm (1 inch) pieces

1 tablespoon sugar

6 new potatoes, halved

salt and pepper

2 tablespoons chives, finely chopped, to garnish

Heat the oil in a large flameproof casserole, add the veal and, turning the pieces frequently, cook them for about 10 minutes until evenly brown. Sprinkle the flour over the meat. Continue cooking, stirring frequently, for 5 minutes until the flour is brown.

Add the garlic and cook gently for 30 seconds, and then pour in the stock and stir well. Add the tomato purée, parsley, thyme and bay leaf and season with salt and pepper. Cover and simmer over a medium-low heat for 30 minutes.

Melt the butter in a large frying pan, add the onions and carrots and then cook for 5 minutes, stirring occasionally. Sprinkle with the sugar and cook for 5 minutes, stirring constantly. Transfer the vegetables with a slotted spoon to the veal mixture, then cover and cook for 30 minutes.

Add the potatoes to the casserole and cook, covered, for 30 minutes. Adjust the seasoning if necessary, then sprinkle with the chives and serve immediately with a selection of green vegetables.

Serves 6

left: *beef rouladen*
below: *veal ragoût*

Bacon and Potato Hot Pot

20 g (¾ oz) butter, for greasing
750 g (1½ lb) potatoes, thickly sliced
500 g (1 lb) thickly sliced smoked
   bacon, rinded
2 tablespoons parsley, chopped
2 onions, thinly sliced
600 ml (1 pint) chicken stock
salt and pepper

Grease a large casserole dish with 1 tablespoon of the butter. Place one-third of the potato slices on the bottom of the dish and season with a little salt and pepper. Top with half of the bacon rashers.

Sprinkle half of the parsley over the bacon and add half of the onion slices. Season lightly with salt and pepper. Arrange one-third of the potato slices over the top and season lightly again.

Repeat the layers with the rest of the bacon, parsley and onion slices and put the remaining potatoes in an overlapping layer on top.

Pour the stock into the casserole dish. Grease a sheet of greaseproof paper with the remaining butter and use to cover the casserole.

Cover with a lid and then cook in a preheated oven, 120°C (250°F), Gas Mark ½, for 1½ hours.

Remove the lid and greaseproof paper and return the casserole to the oven for 20–30 minutes until the top is golden brown.

Serves 4–6

Baked Bean Casserole

4 rashers of streaky bacon, rinded
2 onions, finely chopped
2 green peppers, cored, deseeded
   and chopped
2 x 500 g (1 lb) cans baked beans in
   tomato sauce
8 frankfurters, cut into 5 cm (2 inch)
   lengths
1 tablespoon Worcestershire sauce
2 tablespoons demerara sugar
1 teaspoon prepared mustard
salt and pepper

Cook the bacon in a large frying pan over a moderate heat, turning frequently, until crisp. Drain on kitchen paper and then crumble the bacon. Set aside.

Heat the bacon drippings in the frying pan over a moderate heat. Add the onions and green peppers and cook for 5 minutes, stirring frequently. Remove the pan from the heat.

In a large bowl, combine the bacon, onions, green peppers, baked

beans, frankfurters, Worcestershire sauce, sugar, mustard and season with salt and pepper. Stir well and transfer the mixture to a medium casserole dish. Cook the casserole, uncovered, in a preheated oven, 160°C (325°F), Gas Mark 3, for 30 minutes until heated through. Serve the casserole with toast and a cooked green vegetable.

Serves 6

Braised Stuffed Pork Chops

6 pork chops, about 175 g (6 oz)
    each, 2.5 cm (1 inch) thick, and fat
    trimmed
125 g (4 oz) dried breadcrumbs
1 small onion, finely chopped
1 celery stick, finely sliced
1 garlic clove, finely chopped
2 tablespoons parsley, finely chopped
1 egg, beaten
¼ teaspoon paprika
2 tablespoons vegetable oil
650 ml (1¼ pints) chicken stock
125 ml (4 fl oz) white wine
2 tablespoons cornflour
125 ml (4 fl oz) double or whipping
    cream
salt and pepper
bunch of watercress, to garnish

Cut a pocket in the side of each pork chop for the stuffing, but do not cut all the way through the chop. Sprinkle the chops with salt and pepper and set aside while you prepare the stuffing.

Combine the breadcrumbs, onion, celery, garlic, parsley, beaten egg and paprika in a large bowl and season with salt and pepper. Stuff the pork chops with this mixture. Use some metal skewers or wooden cocktail sticks to enclose the stuffing and then set aside.

Heat the oil in a flameproof casserole and cook the pork chops on one side for 6–7 minutes until brown. Turn the chops over and cook for 4–5 minutes on the other side. Remove from the casserole and set aside. Drain the excess fat from the casserole and discard.

Add 600 ml (1 pint) of the stock together with the white wine to the casserole, scraping the bottom to incorporate all the bits. Bring to the boil and then return the pork chops to the casserole. Cover and cook in a preheated oven, 180°C (350°F), Gas Mark 4, for 1¼ hours.

Remove the casserole from the oven and transfer the chops to a heated serving platter and keep warm. Place the casserole dish over a high heat.

Combine the cornflour and the remaining stock in a cup, stirring until smooth. Using a whisk, blend the cornflour mixture into the liquid in the casserole. Bring to the boil, stirring constantly. Stir the cream into the casserole and adjust the seasoning, if necessary.

To serve, pour the sauce over the pork chops and garnish with the watercress. Creamed potatoes, buttered green beans and apple sauce go well with this dish.

Serves 6

left: bacon and potato hot pot
above: *braised stuffed pork chops*

Lamb with Lemon-Dill Sauce

4 slices from a shank end of lamb,
about 250 g (8 oz) each

2 garlic cloves, cut into 16 thin slices
each

50 g (2 oz) plain flour

25 ml (1 fl oz) vegetable oil

1 onion, thinly sliced

2 celery sticks, thinly sliced

1 tablespoon thyme leaves

1 x 5 cm (2 inch) piece of lemon rind

1 bay leaf

450 ml (¾ pint) chicken or lamb stock

3 eggs, beaten

85 ml (3 fl oz) lemon juice

3 tablespoons finely chopped dill

salt and pepper

To garnish:

lemon slices, halved

dill sprigs

Make 8 small incisions in each slice of lamb and insert 1 slice of garlic into each incision. Put the flour, salt and pepper on a large plate, coat the lamb in the seasoned flour, and then shake off the excess.

Heat the oil in a large flameproof casserole, add the lamb and cook for 10 minutes, turning frequently. Transfer to a plate and set aside.

Add the onion, celery, thyme, lemon rind and bay leaf to the casserole. Cook over a moderate heat for about 5 minutes. Blend in the stock and bring to the boil.

Add the lamb shank pieces to the casserole, then cover and cook in a preheated oven, 160°C (325°F), Gas Mark 3, for 1 hour or until tender.

To make the sauce combine the eggs and lemon juice in a bowl. Whisk in 250 ml (8 fl oz) of strained liquid from the casserole, return to a saucepan and cook over a low heat, stirring constantly. Add the dill, salt and pepper.

Remove the lemon rind and bay leaf before serving the lamb with halved lemon slices and dill sprigs.

Serves 4

above: lamb with lemon-dill sauce
right: braised shank end of lamb with bouquet of vegetables

Braised Shank End of Lamb with Bouquet of Vegetables

4 pieces of shank end (or knuckle) of lamb, about 375 g (12 oz) each

1 tablespoon thyme

50 g (2 oz) butter

2 tablespoons oil

1 onion, finely chopped

600 ml (1 pint) dry white wine

600 ml (1 pint) chicken or lamb stock

2 carrots, diced

2 celery sticks, diced

4 tablespoons cornflour

50 ml (2 fl oz) dry white wine

125 g (4 oz) frozen peas, thawed, or cooked fresh peas

salt and pepper

Sprinkle the lamb with the thyme and season with salt and pepper. Heat the butter and oil in a large flameproof casserole. Add the lamb and onion and cook, turning frequently, for 10 minutes until the shanks are brown.

Add the wine and stock to the casserole and cook in a preheated oven, 160°C (325°F), Gas Mark 3, for 1½ hours until tender. Cover the casserole if the liquid seems to be reducing too quickly.

Remove the lamb shanks from the casserole and cut the meat from the bone into bite-sized pieces. Skim the fat from the liquid, then add the meat, carrots and celery and cook over a medium-high heat for 15 minutes, stirring occasionally.

Combine the cornflour and white wine in a cup until smooth. Using a whisk, stir into the casserole. Cook, stirring constantly, until smooth and thick. Add the peas and cook for 3–4 minutes.

To serve, transfer the lamb mixture to a heated serving platter and serve immediately.

Serves 4

Cod and Cheddar Casserole

50 g (2 oz) butter

1 onion, finely chopped

125 g (4 oz) button mushrooms, cleaned and sliced

50 g (2 oz) plain flour

350 ml (12 fl oz) milk

50 ml (2 fl oz) dry white wine

175 g (6 oz) Cheddar cheese, grated

750 g (1½ lb) thick cod or haddock fillets, skinned

1 red pepper, cored, deseeded and diced

salt and pepper

Topping:

50 g (2 oz) self-raising flour

50 g (2 oz) soft white breadcrumbs

2 tablespoons shredded suet

1 tablespoon parsley, finely chopped

2 teaspoons lemon rind, finely grated

1 egg, beaten

Melt the butter in a large saucepan over a moderate heat. Add the onion and mushrooms and cook for 10 minutes, stirring occasionally. Blend in the flour and then cook for 2–3 minutes, stirring frequently.

Using a whisk, gradually stir in the milk and white wine. Bring the sauce to the boil, then simmer for 2–3 minutes until smooth and thick. Add the cheese, season with salt and pepper and cook until the cheese has just melted. Remove the sauce from the heat and set aside.

Place the fish fillets in a large casserole and sprinkle with the red pepper, then pour the sauce over the top. Set aside.

To make the topping, mix the flour, breadcrumbs, suet, parsley and lemon rind in a large bowl and season with salt and pepper. Make a well in the centre of the mixture and add the beaten egg. Drawing in the flour mixture from the sides, quickly combine the dough.

Shape the mixture into 8 balls and place the balls on top of the fish. Cover and cook in a preheated oven, 200°C (400°F), Gas Mark 6, for 20 minutes or until the topping is cooked and the fish flakes easily.

Serves 4–6

Haddock with Cider and Vegetables

250 ml (8 fl oz) dry cider

2 onions, thinly sliced

750 g (1½ lb) boneless, skinless haddock fillets, cut into 10 cm (4 inch) pieces

1 green pepper, cored, deseeded and diced

3 tomatoes, skinned, deseeded and chopped

1 tablespoon parsley, finely chopped

1 tablespoon marjoram, finely chopped

4 tablespoons fresh white breadcrumbs

25 g (1 oz) Parmesan cheese, freshly
   grated
salt and pepper
To garnish:
2 lemon wedges
1 large sprig of parsley

Put the cider in a saucepan over a
high heat and then bring to the
boil. Reduce the heat and add the
onions. Simmer for 5 minutes or
until the cider has reduced by one-
quarter. Remove from the heat.

Place the fish in a flameproof
casserole. Stir in the cider mixture,
green pepper, tomatoes, parsley and
marjoram and season with salt and
pepper. Cover the casserole and
bring to the boil.

Place the casserole in a preheated
oven, 160°C (325°F), Gas Mark 3,
and cook for 15 minutes or until
the fish flakes easily.

Combine the breadcrumbs and
Parmesan in a small bowl. Remove
the casserole from the oven and
then sprinkle with the breadcrumb
mixture. Place under a preheated
grill and cook for 2–3 minutes until
browned. Garnish with the lemon
wedges and parsley sprigs and serve
immediately.

Serves 4–6

*left: haddock with cider and
vegetables*
*right: prawn, garlic and herb
casserole*

Prawn, Garlic and Herb Casserole

125 ml (4 fl oz) olive oil
125 ml (4 fl oz) dry white vermouth
   or dry white wine
85 ml (3 fl oz) lemon juice
4 garlic cloves, finely chopped
15 g (½ oz) parsley, finely chopped
2½ tablespoons oregano, finely
   chopped
750 g (1½ lb) large uncooked prawns,
   peeled, deveined and tails left
   intact
salt and pepper
To garnish:
4 lemon twists
4 sprigs of parsley

Combine the oil, vermouth or wine,
lemon juice, garlic, parsley and
oregano in a saucepan. Bring to the
boil, stirring frequently, and then
remove from the heat and season to
taste with salt and pepper. Set aside
and cool for 30 minutes.

Arrange the prawns in a single
layer in a flameproof casserole dish.
Pour the vermouth mixture over the
top. Cover the casserole and leave
to marinate at room temperature for
about 1 hour.

Place the casserole in a preheated
oven, 190°C (375°F), Gas Mark 5,
and cook for 10–15 minutes until
the prawns are pink and firm.

Remove the prawns from the
casserole, arrange them on a heated
serving platter and keep warm. Boil
the cooking liquid until reduced
and thickened. Pour the sauce over
the prawns and serve immediately,
garnished with the lemon twists
and parsley sprigs.

Serves 4

Quick Dishes

Chicken, Tomato and Olive Casserole

3 tablespoons olive or vegetable oil
8 chicken thighs, about 150 g (5 oz)
  each
2 large onions, chopped
1 large garlic clove, finely chopped
3 small red peppers, cored, deseeded
  and cut into strips
6 tomatoes, skinned, deseeded and
  chopped

125 g (4 oz) ham, diced
75 g (3 oz) green olives, pitted
300 ml (½ pint) chicken stock
salt and pepper
1 bunch watercress, to garnish
  (optional)

Heat the oil in a large flameproof casserole, add the chicken thighs and cook, turning frequently, for 10 minutes until brown on all sides. Remove the chicken and drain on kitchen paper. Set aside.

Pour off all but 1 tablespoon of the fat in the casserole. Add the onions and garlic and cook over a moderate heat for about 5 minutes. Add the peppers and tomatoes and then cook for 10 minutes. Stir in the ham and olives.

Place the chicken pieces on top of the vegetable mixture. Sprinkle with salt and pepper and pour in the stock. Cover and simmer gently for 40 minutes until the chicken is cooked through.

Transfer the chicken with a slotted spoon to a heated serving platter and keep warm. Turn up the heat and continue cooking the sauce in the casserole, uncovered, for about 5 minutes until thickened.

Pour the sauce over the chicken. Garnish with the watercress, if liked, and serve immediately with some steamed rice or crusty bread.

Serves 4

Gingered Citrus Chicken

4 x 150 g (5 oz) boneless, skinless chicken breasts

½ teaspoon paprika

25 g (1 oz) butter

175 ml (6 fl oz) orange juice

50 ml (2 fl oz) lemon juice

grated rind of 1 lemon

1 teaspoon peeled fresh ginger root, finely chopped

2 teaspoons cornflour

2 tablespoons chicken stock

salt and pepper

To garnish:

2 tablespoons slivered almonds, toasted

4 lemon twists

4 sprigs of parsley

Sprinkle the chicken breasts with the paprika and a little salt and pepper, then set aside.

Melt the butter in a flameproof casserole and add the chicken breasts. Cook for 5–10 minutes, turning frequently, until brown on both sides. Drain off the excess fat.

Blend in the orange and lemon juices, the lemon rind and ginger. Cover the casserole and cook in a preheated oven, 180°C (350°F), Gas Mark 4, for 25–30 minutes until the chicken is cooked.

Remove the chicken breasts from the casserole and place on a heated serving platter. Keep warm.

Pour the juice mixture into a small saucepan and heat through gently. Combine the cornflour and stock in a small cup until smooth. Using a whisk, stir into the juice mixture. Cook, stirring constantly, until the mixture comes to the boil. Cook for 1 minute, still stirring, until thick and smooth.

To serve, coat the chicken pieces with the citrus sauce. Sprinkle with the almonds and garnish with the lemon twists and parsley sprigs.

Serves 4

left: chicken, tomato and olive casserole
above: gingered citrus chicken

Orange and Pineapple Chicken

1 x 2 kg (4 lb) chicken, quartered

2 tablespoons vegetable oil

25 g (1 oz) butter

175 ml (6 fl oz) orange juice

2 x 250 g (8 oz) cans pineapple
    chunks, juice reserved

3 lemon slices

50 g (2 oz) skinned almonds, toasted

salt and pepper

sprigs of flat-leaf parsley, to garnish

Season the chicken quarters with salt and pepper. Heat the oil and butter in a flameproof casserole, add the chicken, skin-side down, and then brown for 10 minutes, turning frequently. Transfer the chicken to a plate and set aside.

Drain off the excess fat from the casserole and add the orange juice. Scraping the casserole bottom to incorporate all the bits, bring to a simmer. Return the chicken to the casserole, coating with the orange juice mixture.

Cover the casserole and cook in a preheated oven, 180°C (350°F), Gas Mark 4, for 25 minutes. Add the drained pineapple chunks together with 125 ml (4 fl oz) of pineapple juice and the lemon slices. Cover the casserole and return to the oven for 15 minutes.

Add the remaining pineapple juice – about 125 ml (4 fl oz) – and almonds to the casserole. Return to the oven and then cook, uncovered, for 5 minutes.

Arrange the chicken on a heated serving platter. Pour the sauce over the top and then garnish with the parsley. Serve with steamed rice and stir-fried green vegetables.

Serves 4

Chicken Noodle Casserole with Almonds

2.75 litres (5 pints) water
1 tablespoon olive oil
500 g (1 lb) fettuccine verdi
salt
Casserole:
50 g (2 oz) butter plus extra for
  greasing
1 shallot, finely chopped
4 tablespoons plain flour
250 ml (8 fl oz) double cream
475 ml (16 fl oz) chicken stock
1 tablespoon parsley, chopped
500 g (1 lb) cooked chicken meat,
  cubed

50 g (2 oz) slivered almonds, toasted
salt and pepper

Bring the water, oil and salt to the boil in a large saucepan and add the noodles. Cook for 5–7 minutes, or according to the instructions on the packet, until the noodles are just tender. Drain and rinse in a colander.

Meanwhile, melt the butter in a pan and add the shallot. Cook for about 4 minutes until softened, then blend in the flour. Cook for 2–3 minutes, stirring all the time. Using a whisk, gradually stir in the cream and stock. Cook, stirring constantly, until smooth and thick. Remove the sauce from the heat, stir in the parsley and season with salt and pepper. Set aside.

Grease a casserole with the butter and arrange the noodles evenly on the bottom. Cover with the chicken and sprinkle half of the almonds evenly over the top. Pour the sauce over the mixture and cook, covered, in a preheated oven, 180°C (350°F), Gas Mark 4, for 20 minutes.

Remove the casserole from the oven and serve garnished with the remaining almonds.

Serves 4–6

left: orange-pineapple chicken
below: *chicken noodle casserole with almonds*

Meanwhile, melt the butter in a flameproof casserole, add the onions and cook for 10 minutes, stirring frequently. Sprinkle the flour over the onions and stir well to combine. Cook for 2–3 minutes, stirring constantly. Using a whisk, gradually stir in the stock and cream. Cook for 5 minutes, stirring, until smooth and thick.

Mix the potatoes, corned beef, beetroots, salt and pepper and add to the casserole. Cover and cook gently for 20 minutes. Remove the casserole from the heat and uncover. Serve garnished with watercress.

Serves 4

Spicy Beef and Bean Casserole

You could serve this spicy casserole with a selection of tortillas, guacamole and salad garnishes, such as shredded lettuce, tomatoes and spring onions, plus some more hot sauce to make it a really substantial meal.

500 g (1 lb) lean minced beef
1 onion, chopped
1 green pepper, cored, deseeded and chopped
1 garlic clove, finely chopped
425 g (14 oz) can tomatoes
425 g (14 oz) can kidney beans, drained
425 g (14 oz) can butter beans, not drained

Red Flannel Hash

This is a time-honoured dish, originating in France as hache or hachis, which means something cut up. Usually it consists of a mixture of cooked meat, vegetables and gravy, seasoned and then served. Hache crossed the Channel as hash; Samuel Pepys wrote in his diary of having a hash of rabbits. Continuing its journey westwards, hash eventually arrived in North America. This popular hash recipe uses corned beef, potatoes and beetroot. The beetroot colours the dish red – hence its name.

4 potatoes, diced
1.2 litres (2 pints) water
40 g (1½ oz) butter
2 onions, chopped
4 tablespoons plain flour
900 ml (1½ pints) beef stock
75 ml (3 fl oz) double cream
750 g (1½ lb) corned beef, trimmed and diced
12 small cooked beetroots, trimmed and diced
salt and pepper
sprigs of watercress, to garnish

Put the potatoes and water in a pan and bring to the boil, then simmer for 15 minutes until the potatoes are just tender. Drain in a colander.

250 ml (8 fl oz) tomato sauce
150 g (5 oz) can tomato purée
2 teaspoons chilli powder
salt and pepper
125 g (4 oz) Cheddar cheese, grated,
  to garnish

Place the minced beef, onion, green pepper and garlic in a flameproof casserole. Cook over a moderate heat, stirring frequently to break up the meat, for 10 minutes or until the meat is no longer pink. Drain off the excess fat and then mix in the remaining ingredients except the cheese.

Cover the casserole and simmer gently for 30 minutes, stirring occasionally. Sprinkle with the grated cheese just before serving.

Serves 6

---

left: red flannel hash
above: spicy beef and bean casserole
right: boeuf ragoût

Boeuf Ragoût

---

40 g (1½ oz) butter
1 large onion, thinly sliced
1 garlic clove, finely chopped
300 g (10 oz) cooked lean beef,
  cubed
2 carrots, diced
1 potato, diced
350 ml (12 fl oz) beef stock
175 ml (6 fl oz) gravy
2 teaspoons red wine vinegar

salt and pepper
To finish:
2 tablespoons cornflour
50 ml (2 fl oz) red wine or beef stock

Melt the butter in a flameproof casserole over a moderate heat. Add the onion and cook for 8 minutes, stirring frequently. Add the garlic and cook for 2 minutes, stirring frequently.

Add the beef, carrots, potato, beef stock, gravy, vinegar, salt and pepper to the casserole. Bring to the boil, then cover and reduce the heat to moderate. Simmer gently for 25 minutes, stirring occasionally.

Combine the cornflour and wine in a cup until smooth. Using a whisk, stir into the ragoût. Bring the mixture to the boil, stirring constantly until the sauce is smooth and thick. Serve with buttered tagliatelle.

Serves 2–3

Orange and Liver Casserole

The liver should be very thinly sliced. Fresh liver is often not sliced thinly enough, so you may prefer to buy frozen liver. When it is partially thawed, carefully slice it with a sharp knife.

25 g (1 oz) plain flour
1 kg (2 lb) lambs' liver, thinly
   sliced
40 g (1½ oz) butter
2 tablespoons vegetable oil
1 onion, thinly sliced
1 garlic clove, finely chopped
2 oranges, thinly sliced and seeds
   removed
250 ml (8 fl oz) dry red wine
250 ml (8 fl oz) orange juice
2 tablespoons orange marmalade
2 tablespoons thyme leaves
2 tablespoons double cream
salt and pepper
1 tablespoon parsley, finely chopped,
   to garnish

Combine the flour with some salt and pepper on a large plate. Coat the liver with the seasoned flour, shaking off the excess. Set aside.

Heat the butter and oil in a large frying pan, add the onion and garlic and cook for 5 minutes, stirring occasionally. Transfer the onion and garlic to a casserole and set aside.

Add the liver slices to the frying pan. Cook on one side for 2–3 minutes until brown, then turn the slices over. Cook on the other side

for 2 minutes. Transfer the liver with a slotted spoon to the casserole and set aside.

Add the orange slices to the frying pan. Cook for 1–2 minutes, turning frequently. Remove from the pan and arrange over the liver in the casserole.

Add the red wine, orange juice, marmalade and thyme to the frying pan. Season with salt and pepper and bring to the boil, stirring constantly. Remove from the heat and pour over the ingredients in the casserole.

Cover the casserole and cook in a preheated oven, 140°C (275°F), Gas Mark 1, for 30 minutes. Remove from the oven and then stir in the cream. Serve hot, garnished with chopped parsley.

Serves 6

Cider Pork Chops

4 x 175 g (6 oz) loin pork chops
2 tablespoons vegetable oil
15 g (½ oz) butter
1 onion, thinly sliced
1 cooking apple, peeled, cored and
   chopped
250 g (8 oz) button mushrooms,
   sliced
1 large garlic clove, finely chopped
1 tablespoon thyme leaves
1 tablespoon rosemary, finely
   chopped
350 ml (12 fl oz) dry cider
150 ml (¼ pint) double cream
salt and pepper

Season the pork chops with salt and pepper. Heat the oil and butter in a flameproof casserole, add the pork chops and brown on both sides for 10 minutes, turning frequently. Remove the chops from the casserole and set aside.

Add the onion, apple, mushrooms and garlic to the casserole. Cook over a moderate heat for 5 minutes, stirring frequently. Push the mixture to one side and return the chops to the casserole. Stir in the thyme and rosemary and spoon the onion mixture over the chops. Add the cider and reduce the heat to low. Cover the casserole and simmer gently for 45 minutes.

Transfer the chops to a heated serving platter and keep warm. Raise the heat under the casserole to moderate and stir in the cream. Bring the sauce to a simmer and let it reduce slightly, stirring frequently. Taste the sauce and adjust the seasoning, if necessary.

Pour the sauce over the pork chops and serve immediately with creamed potatoes and red cabbage.

Serves 4

Paprika
Pork Chops

25 g (1 oz) plain flour
2 tablespoons Hungarian paprika
¼ teaspoon cayenne pepper
4 x 175 g (6 oz) loin pork chops
1 tablespoon vegetable oil

4 potatoes, thinly sliced
1 large onion, thinly sliced
300 ml (½ pint) beef stock
salt and pepper
To thicken:
300 ml (½ pint) soured cream
2 tablespoons plain flour
To garnish:
1 bunch watercress
1 teaspoon caraway seeds (optional)

Combine the flour with the paprika, cayenne pepper, salt and pepper on a large plate. Coat the pork chops in this mixture and set aside.

Heat the oil in a large flameproof casserole, add the pork chops and brown for 10 minutes, turning frequently. Remove the chops and then set aside.

Lay the potatoes and onion slices in the bottom of the casserole. Place the pork chops on top of the slices. Pour the stock into the casserole.

Cover and cook in a preheated oven, 190°C (375°F), Gas Mark 5, for 45 minutes.

Combine the soured cream and flour until smooth, and set aside. Remove the pork chops and vegetables from the casserole. Arrange on a heated serving platter and keep warm. Place the casserole over a medium-low heat and, using a whisk, stir in the soured cream mixture. Cook until just heated through. Remove the sauce from the heat and pour over the chops. Garnish with the watercress and caraway seeds, if using, and serve immediately.

Serves 4

left: orange and liver casserole
below: cider pork chops

Calf's Liver with Mushrooms and Olives

15 g (½ oz) butter, for greasing

1 kg (2 lb) thinly sliced calf's liver

125 g (4 oz) button mushrooms, sliced

125 g (4 oz) ripe olives, pitted

1 onion, chopped

1 green pepper, cored, deseeded and chopped

1 garlic clove, finely chopped

2 x 425 g (14 oz) cans tomatoes

125 ml (4 fl oz) tomato ketchup

50 ml (2 fl oz) beef stock

2 tablespoons oregano, finely chopped

1 tablespoon parsley, finely chopped

2 tablespoons olive oil

1 tablespoon plain flour

salt and pepper

Grease a large casserole with the butter. Place the liver slices in the casserole and set aside.

Place the mushrooms, olives, onion, green pepper, garlic, canned tomatoes, ketchup, stock, oregano and parsley in a large bowl, season with salt and pepper and mix until well blended. Mix together the oil and flour in a cup until smooth and then stir into the sauce mixture.

Pour the sauce over the liver slices and place the casserole in a preheated oven, 180°C (350°F), Gas Mark 4. Cook for 30–40 minutes until tender. Serve with rice and a vegetable of your choice.

Serves 6

Frankfurter and Vegetable Casserole

2 tablespoons vegetable oil
1 large onion, thinly sliced
1 green pepper, cored, deseeded and cubed
1 red pepper, cored, deseeded and cubed
1 garlic clove, crushed
1 green chilli, deseeded and finely chopped
2 x 425 g (14 oz) cans tomatoes
1 tablespoon demerara sugar
8 frankfurters
salt and pepper

Heat the oil in a large flameproof casserole and add the onion. Cook for 5 minutes, stirring frequently.

Add the peppers, garlic and chilli and cook for 5 minutes, stirring occasionally. Stir in the tomatoes with the sugar and season to taste with salt and pepper. Place the frankfurters in the casserole.

Cover the casserole and then cook gently over a very low heat for 30 minutes, stirring occasionally.

Serves 4

Lambs' Kidneys in Red Wine

If your budget can stretch to veal kidneys, try substituting them for the lambs' kidneys. Although pre-soaking is not necessary, the white core should be removed. Veal kidneys should be cut into large slices.

8 lambs' kidneys
900 ml (1½ pints) water
25 g (1 oz) butter
2 tablespoons plain flour
300 ml (½ pint) dry red wine
300 ml (½ pint) beef or lamb stock
3 tablespoons parsley, finely chopped
1 garlic clove, finely chopped
salt and pepper

Place the kidneys in a bowl and cover them with the water. Add a little salt and then leave to soak for about 30 minutes. Drain, remove the skin and cut in half. Remove the white core and set aside.

Melt the butter in a flameproof casserole, add the kidneys and cook for 2–3 minutes, stirring frequently. Sprinkle the flour onto the kidneys and stir well to combine. Gradually stir in the red wine and stock. Bring the sauce to the boil, stirring continuously, and then add the parsley and garlic and season with salt and pepper.

Cover the casserole and cook in a preheated oven, 180°C (350°F), Gas Mark 4, for 30 minutes. Serve with hot buttered toast.

Serves 4

left: calf's liver with mushrooms and olives
above: *frankfurter and vegetable casserole*

Mushroom and Noodle Casserole

3 litres (5 pints) water

375 g (12 oz) fettuccine

75 g (3 oz) butter

1 small onion, finely chopped

500 g (1 lb) small button mushrooms,
  cleaned

2 tablespoons plain flour

350 ml (12 fl oz) double cream

125 ml (4 fl oz) dry white wine

2 eggs, beaten

50 ml (2 fl oz) milk

50 g (2 oz) Parmesan cheese, freshly
  grated

salt and pepper

1 tablespoon chives, finely snipped,
  to garnish

Bring the water to the boil in a large saucepan, then add the fettuccine and cook for 5-7 minutes or according to the instructions on the packet. Drain well in a colander, shaking to remove excess water. Place the fettuccine in a large bowl, then add 2 tablespoons of the butter and toss well to coat. Set aside.

Melt the remaining butter in a large saucepan and cook the onion over a low heat for 5 minutes. Add the mushrooms and season lightly with salt and pepper. Cook for about 5 minutes until tender.

Sprinkle in the flour and cook for 2–3 minutes, stirring constantly.

Using a whisk, gradually stir in the cream and wine. Cook gently for 2–3 minutes, stirring frequently, then remove the pan from the heat.

Combine the eggs and milk in a small bowl until well blended. Using a whisk, slowly stir into the creamed mushroom mixture.

Place the fettuccine in a large casserole and pour the creamed mushroom mixture over the top, then stir to combine. Sprinkle with the Parmesan and cook in a preheated oven, 200°C (400°F), Gas Mark 6, for 20 minutes.

Garnish with the chives and serve the casserole accompanied by a green salad with plenty of tomatoes and French bread.

Serves 8

above: mushroom and noodle casserole
below: sausage and white wine casserole
right: paprikash meatballs

34

Sausage and White Wine Casserole

350 ml (12 fl oz) dry white wine

250 ml (8 fl oz) beef stock

8 small onions, peeled

2 carrots, diced

1 tablespoon Dijon mustard

1 tablespoon vegetable oil

750 g (1½ lb) pork sausages

salt and pepper

1 tablespoon parsley, finely chopped, to garnish

Combine the wine, stock, onions, carrots, mustard, salt and pepper in a casserole. Cover and cook in a preheated oven, 180°C (350°F), Gas Mark 4, for 30 minutes.

Meanwhile, heat the oil in a large frying pan and cook the sausages, turning them frequently, for about 5–7 minutes until brown.

Add the sausages to the casserole and place in the preheated oven. Cook, uncovered, for 30 minutes until the sausages are cooked and the vegetables are tender.

Sprinkle with chopped parsley and serve with creamed potatoes and a large green salad.

Serves 6

Paprikash Meatballs

500 g (1 lb) lean minced beef

1 egg, well beaten

50 g (2 oz) dried breadcrumbs

50 ml (2 fl oz) milk

1½ tablespoons Hungarian paprika

1 tablespoon parsley, finely chopped

2 tablespoons vegetable oil

1 onion, finely chopped

125 g (4 oz) button mushrooms, sliced

350 ml (12 fl oz) beef stock

250 ml (8 fl oz) soured cream

1 tablespoon plain flour

salt and pepper

chervil sprigs, to garnish

Thoroughly combine the minced beef, beaten egg, breadcrumbs, milk, 1 tablespoon paprika and parsley in a large bowl. Season with salt and pepper. Shape the mixture into 24 x 4 cm (1½ inch) balls.

Heat the oil in a flameproof casserole. Add the meatballs and brown for 10 minutes, turning frequently. Remove them from the casserole and set aside. Drain off all but 1 tablespoon of the fat in the casserole.

Add the onion, mushrooms and remaining paprika to the casserole. Cook gently for 5 minutes, stirring frequently. Add the meatballs and blend in the stock. Cover and cook in a preheated oven, 180°C (350°F), Gas Mark 4, for 30 minutes.

Combine the soured cream and flour in a bowl until smooth. Place the casserole over a moderate heat on the hob. Using a whisk, stir the soured cream mixture into the casserole and cook, stirring constantly, for 5 minutes until smooth and thickened. Season to taste with salt and pepper. Serve garnished with sprigs of chervil.

Serves 6

preheated oven, 180°C (350°F), Gas Mark 4. Cook for 30 minutes until golden brown and bubbling.

Serves 4–6

Piquant Tuna and Egg

40 g (1½ oz) butter
40 g (1½ oz) plain flour
350 ml (12 fl oz) milk
2 x 200 g (7 oz) cans tuna, drained
  and broken into chunks
2 hard-boiled eggs, shelled and
  chopped
1 red pepper, cored, deseeded and
  chopped
3 tablespoons parsley, finely
  chopped
2 teaspoons lemon juice
2 teaspoons prepared mustard
½ teaspoon drained prepared
  horseradish
salt and pepper

Melt the butter and blend in the flour. Cook, stirring frequently, for 2–3 minutes, then, using a whisk, gradually stir in the milk and cook, stirring constantly, until the sauce is smooth and thickened. Season with salt and paper, and remove from the heat. Transfer to a large bowl.

Stir in the tuna, eggs, red pepper parsley, lemon juice, mustard and horseradish. Mix lightly together, taking care not to break up the chunks of tuna.

Smoked Haddock and Potato Casserole

4 potatoes, cut into chunks
1.2 litres (2 pints) water
4 tablespoons Greek yogurt
15 g (½ oz) butter
¼ teaspoon nutmeg, freshly grated
salt and pepper
For the haddock:
750 g (1½ lb) smoked haddock
475 ml (16 fl oz) milk
1 bay leaf
50 g (2 oz) butter
50 g (2 oz) plain flour
50 g (2 oz) Cheddar cheese, grated

Put the potatoes and water in a large pan and bring to the boil. Lower the heat and simmer gently for 15–20 minutes until tender.

Drain the potatoes in a colander.

Return the potatoes to the pan and add the yogurt, butter and nutmeg. Mash until smooth and season to taste with salt and pepper. Pipe or spoon the potatoes around the sides of a casserole dish.

Meanwhile, put the haddock, milk and bay leaf in a large saucepan. Cover and simmer gently for 5 minutes. Strain off the cooking liquid and reserve. Discard the bay leaf. Remove the skin from the haddock, then flake the fish.

Melt the butter in the same pan over a moderate heat. Add the flour and cook for 2–3 minutes, stirring constantly. Using a whisk, gradually stir in the reserved cooking liquid. Cook until smooth and thickened. Return the flaked haddock to the sauce, then remove from the heat.

Pour the mixture into the casserole dish, sprinkle with grated Cheddar and place, uncovered, in a

Spoon the tuna mixture into a casserole, then cover and cook in a preheated oven, 180°C (350°F), Gas Mark 4, for 15–20 minutes, until hot and bubbling.

Serves 4

Belgian Fish Casserole

175 ml (6 fl oz) fish stock
125 ml (4 fl oz) dry white wine
2 tablespoons lemon juice
1 tablespoon thyme leaves
1 bay leaf, crushed
25 g (1 oz) butter
2 carrots, cut into matchstick strips
2 leeks, white part only, cut into matchstick strips
1 celery stick, cut into matchstick strips

500 g (1 lb) boneless, skinned cod fillets
salt and pepper
To garnish:
1 tablespoon chives, snipped
4 lemon wedges

Combine the stock, wine, lemon juice, thyme and bay leaf in a bowl. Season lightly with salt and pepper and set aside.

Melt the butter in a flameproof casserole set over a moderate heat.

Add the carrots, leeks and celery and then cook for 5 minutes, stirring frequently. Arrange the fish fillets on top of the vegetables in the casserole and pour the stock mixture over the fish.

Cover the casserole and cook in a preheated oven, 180°C (350°F), Gas Mark 4, for 10–15 minutes or until the fish is cooked and flakes easily when tested with a fork.

Remove the fish to a heated serving platter and keep warm. Boil the vegetable mixture, uncovered, over a moderate heat for 5 minutes or until the liquid is reduced by half. Spoon the vegetable mixture over the fish fillets, garnish with a sprinkling of snipped chives and serve with lemon wedges.

Serves 4

above left: smoked haddock and potato casserole
above: piquant tuna and egg
below: Belgian fish casserole

Creamy Finnan Haddie Casserole

500 g (1 lb) boneless finnan haddock
750 ml (1¼ pints) boiling water
50 g (2 oz) butter
50 g (2 oz) plain flour
350 ml (12 fl oz) single cream
¼ teaspoon paprika
salt (optional) and pepper
75 g (3 oz) Cheddar cheese, grated
25 g (1 oz) soft white breadcrumbs
To garnish:
4 lemon wedges (optional)
sprig of parsley

Place the finnan haddock in a
saucepan and cover with the boiling
water. Simmer over a low heat for
10 minutes until the fish flakes
easily. Drain well and then flake the
fish and set aside.

Melt the butter in a small
saucepan and blend in the flour.
Cook for 2–3 minutes, stirring all
the time. Using a whisk, gradually
stir in the cream and bring the
sauce to a simmer. Cook, stirring
constantly, until thick and smooth.
Remove from the heat, then add the
paprika and season with salt, if
using, and pepper. Stir in the flaked
fish and 50 g (2 oz) grated Cheddar.

Grease a casserole dish and pour
in the fish mixture. Top with the
breadcrumbs and the remaining
grated cheese. Cook, uncovered, in
a preheated oven, 190°C (375°F),
Gas Mark 5, for 20–25 minutes until
the top is browned.

Tuna Carousel

15 g (½ oz) butter, for greasing
200 g (7 oz) can tuna, drained and
   flaked
250 g (8 oz) frozen peas, thawed
125 g (4 oz) button mushrooms, sliced
1 garlic clove, finely chopped
¼ teaspoon dill
¼ teaspoon celery seed
375 g (12 oz) cooked noodles
25 g (1 oz) fresh white breadcrumbs
Sauce:
50 g (2 oz) butter
50 g (2 oz) plain flour
475 ml (16 fl oz) milk
2 tablespoons dry sherry
salt and pepper

Grease a casserole dish with the
butter and add the tuna, peas,
mushrooms, garlic, dill and celery
seed. Stir gently together and set
aside while you make the sauce.

For the sauce, melt the butter in a
saucepan, then add the flour and
cook for 2–3 minutes, stirring
constantly. Using a whisk, gradually
stir in the milk and cook, stirring
constantly, until the sauce is smooth
and thickened. Blend in the sherry
and salt and pepper to taste.

Stir half of the sauce into the
tuna mixture. Spread the noodles
over the tuna and then pour the
remaining sauce over the top.
Sprinkle with the breadcrumbs.

Transfer the uncovered casserole
to a preheated oven, 180°C (350°F),
Gas Mark 4, and then cook for
about 30 minutes until the topping
is crisp and golden.

Serves 2–3

above: tuna carousel
*right: creamy finnan haddie
casserole, salmon corn casserole*

Garnish with the lemon wedges, if liked, and a sprig of parsley. Serve immediately with some toast and a cucumber salad.

Serves 4

Salmon Corn Casserole

25 g (1 oz) butter
3 x 275 g (9 oz) cans cream-style corn
425 g (14 oz) can salmon
3 eggs, beaten
25 g (1 oz) cheese cracker crumbs,
    reserving 1 tablespoon for topping
salt and pepper
To garnish:
lemon wedges
sprigs of parsley

Grease a large casserole dish with 1 tablespoon of the butter. Combine the corn, salmon, eggs and cracker crumbs in a large bowl and season with salt and pepper. Transfer the mixture to the casserole, top with the reserved cracker crumbs and dot with the remaining butter.

Place the uncovered casserole in a preheated oven, 180°C (350°F), Gas Mark 4, and cook for 1 hour. Serve piping hot, garnished with lemon wedges and parsley.

Serves 6

Classic Dishes

Chilli Chicken

4 chicken portions
1 tablespoon oil
25 g (1 oz) butter
1 onion, chopped
1 small green pepper, cored,
   deseeded and roughly chopped
1 small red pepper, cored, deseeded
   and roughly chopped
3 teaspoons chilli powder
1 tablespoon plain flour
425 g (14 oz) can tomatoes
dash of Tabasco sauce (optional)
salt and pepper
freshly cooked rice, to serve
To garnish:
paprika
1 teaspoon poppy seeds
1 teaspoon parsley, chopped

Trim the chicken portions and then sprinkle lightly with salt and pepper. Heat the oil and butter in a pan and fry the chicken until browned all over. Drain over the pan and transfer to a casserole.

Add the onion and green and red peppers to the pan and cook over a gentle heat for about 2–3 minutes. Sprinkle in the chilli powder and plain flour and stir well. Gradually stir in the tomatoes, then bring to the boil and simmer for 1 minute, stirring. If liked, add Tabasco sauce.

Pour the prepared sauce over the chicken portions in the casserole. Cover closely with a lid or foil and cook in a preheated oven, 180°C (350°F), Gas Mark 4, for 45 minutes.

Uncover and continue cooking for a further 15 minutes or until the chicken is tender and the sauce has thickened. Skim any fat from the surface of the casserole.

Arrange the chicken and sauce on a hot serving dish and surround with a border of freshly cooked rice. As a finishing touch, sprinkle the rice with paprika, poppy seeds and chopped parsley.

Serves 4

Duck with Walnut Sauce

1 x 2.25–2.75 kg (5–6 lb) duckling
1 onion, finely chopped
1 garlic clove, crushed (optional)
50 g (2 oz) walnut pieces,
   chopped
300 ml (½ pint) duckling stock,
   prepared from the giblets
2 tablespoons honey
2 teaspoons cornflour
2 tablespoons cream sherry
1 teaspoon soy sauce
1 tablespoon lemon juice
salt and pepper
To garnish:
25 g (1 oz) walnut halves
1 tablespoon duck dripping
sprigs of watercress

Pat the duckling dry inside and out with kitchen paper and remove any

excess fat. Prick the skin all over with a fork, place in a deep casserole and sprinkle with salt and pepper.

Cook in a preheated oven, 200°C (400°F), Gas Mark 6, for 30 minutes, then drain the dripping from the casserole and reserve.

Heat 1 tablespoon of the duck dripping in a pan and gently fry the onion and garlic for 2–3 minutes until tender. Add the chopped walnuts and continue cooking for 2 minutes. Stir in the strained stock. Check the seasoning and pour the sauce around the duckling.

Cover the casserole with a lid or foil and then return to the oven for 45 minutes. Uncover the casserole, coat the skin of the duck with the honey and cook, uncovered, for 15–20 minutes or until it is tender and the skin is well browned.

Meanwhile, fry the walnut halves in 1 tablespoon of duck dripping until lightly browned, then drain well on kitchen paper.

Transfer the duck to a hot serving dish. Skim off any fat from the sauce in the casserole. Blend the cornflour and sherry, and stir in the

soy sauce and lemon juice. Add a little of the hot liquid from the casserole, blend and then return this mixture to the casserole, stirring briskly. Bring to the boil, then reduce the heat and simmer for 1 minute, stirring.

Garnish the duck with the fried walnuts and watercress and serve the sauce separately.

Serves 5–6

left: chilli chicken
above: *duck with walnut sauce*

Quail Casserole

Although game is traditionally eaten high or hung for a period of time, quail must be eaten fresh. High quail can have a powerful smell that is not very appetizing.

1.2 litres (2 pints) water
250 g (8 oz) bacon, derinded and cut
    into strips
75 g (3 oz) butter
8 quail, about 125 g (4 oz) each
475 ml (16 fl oz) chicken stock
250 ml (8 fl oz) Madeira wine
300 g (10 oz) button mushrooms,
    quartered
15 g (½ oz) dried porcini mushrooms,
    reconstituted in 250 ml (8 fl oz)
    warm water for 30 minutes, drained
    and chopped
3 tablespoons cornflour
125 ml (4 fl oz) double or whipping
    cream
salt and pepper

Boil the water and add the bacon. Cook for 1–2 minutes, then remove the pan from the heat, drain the bacon in a colander and set aside.

Melt 50 g (2 oz) of the butter in a flameproof casserole, add the bacon and, stirring occasionally, cook for 10 minutes. Add the quail to the casserole and brown on all sides, turning frequently. Drain off the excess fat and discard. Blend in the stock and 125 ml (4 fl oz) of the Madeira and season with salt and pepper. Cover the casserole and cook gently for 30 minutes.

While the quail are cooking, melt the remaining butter in a large frying pan and cook the button and porcini mushrooms, covered, for about 10 minutes, shaking the pan frequently. Remove from the heat and set aside.

When the quail have been cooking for 30 minutes, add the fried mushrooms to the casserole Cover and continue cooking for 20 minutes.

Transfer the quail to a heated serving platter and keep them warm. Increase the heat under the casserole to high. Combine the cornflour and remaining Madeira in a cup until smooth. Using a whisk, stir into the casserole. Add the cream and let the mixture come to the boil. Boil for 2–3 minutes, then remove from the heat. Pour the sauce over the quail and serve.

Serves 4

Pheasant and Port Casserole

Porcini mushrooms are dried Italian mushrooms. If they are unavailable, substitute an additional 250 g (8 oz) field mushrooms.

2 pheasants, about 1.25 kg (2½ lb)
    each, skinned and jointed
75 g (3 oz) butter

15 g (½ oz) dried porcini mushrooms, reconstituted in 250 ml (8 fl oz) warm water for 30 minutes, drained and chopped

250 g (8 oz) field mushrooms, cleaned and sliced

25 g (1 oz) plain flour

300 ml (½ pint) pheasant or chicken stock

150 ml (¼ pint) double cream

1 tablespoon parsley, finely chopped, to garnish

Marinade:

450 ml (¾ pint) port wine

1 large onion, sliced

1 large carrot, thinly sliced

2 celery sticks, chopped

1 garlic clove, finely chopped

1 tablespoon thyme leaves

4 juniper berries, crushed

1 bay leaf, crumbled

salt and pepper

Combine the port, onion, carrot, celery, garlic, thyme, juniper berries and bay leaf in a deep bowl and season with salt and pepper. Add the pheasants and turn to coat evenly with the marinade. Cover and chill overnight.

Remove the pheasants from the marinade and then pat dry with kitchen paper. Strain and reserve the marinade.

Heat 50 g (2 oz) of the butter in a frying pan and add the pheasant pieces. Cook, turning occasionally, for 10 minutes until golden brown. Transfer to a flameproof casserole.

Melt the remaining butter in the frying pan and add the porcini and field mushrooms. Cook gently for 5 minutes. Blend in the flour and, stirring continuously, cook for about 2–3 minutes, then lower the

heat. Using a whisk, gradually add the stock and reserved marinade. Continue whisking until the sauce comes to the boil and thickens. Pour over the pheasant pieces.

Cover and cook in a preheated oven, 180°C (350°F), Gas Mark 4, for 1 hour. Transfer the pheasants to a serving dish and keep warm.

Pour the sauce into a saucepan. Bring to the boil, add the cream and simmer for 2–3 minutes. Pour over the pheasants and serve, garnished with parsley. Crisp potato pancakes and steamed broccoli go well with this dish.

Serves 6

left: quail casserole
below: pheasant and port casserole

Casserole of Duck with Red Cabbage

3 tablespoons plain flour

1 x 2.25 kg (4½ lb) duckling, skinned and cut into serving pieces

50 g (2 oz) butter

2 tablespoons vegetable oil

1 large onion, finely chopped

125 ml (4 fl oz) chicken stock

1 tablespoon basil, chopped

½ head red cabbage, about 750 g (1½ lb), cored and finely shredded

1 cooking apple, peeled, cored and chopped

1 garlic clove, finely chopped

3 tablespoons red wine vinegar

2 tablespoons brown sugar

salt and pepper

4 sprigs of parsley, to garnish

Place the flour on a large plate and season with salt and pepper. Toss the duckling pieces thoroughly in the seasoned flour, shaking off the excess, and then set aside.

Melt 25 g (1 oz) of the butter and the oil in a large frying pan and cook the duck for 5–10 minutes, shaking the pan frequently, until browned. Turn the pieces over and continue cooking for 5–10 minutes until browned. Remove the duckling from the pan and drain on kitchen paper. Transfer the duckling pieces to a large casserole.

Add the onion to the frying pan and cook for 10 minutes, stirring frequently, until soft. Transfer the onion to the casserole, then add the chicken stock and basil.

Melt the remaining butter in the frying pan and add the red cabbage. Cook for 10 minutes, stirring occasionally, then stir in the apple, garlic, vinegar and sugar. Season with salt and pepper and simmer for 5 minutes, stirring frequently. Add the cabbage to the casserole.

Cover and cook in a preheated oven, 180°C (350°F), Gas Mark 4, for 1 hour until the duckling is tender. Remove the casserole from the oven and check the seasoning. Place the cabbage on a large heated serving platter and top with the duckling pieces. Garnish with parsley sprigs.

Serves 4

Civet de Canard

1 x 2 kg (4 lb) duckling, quartered

50 g (2 oz) plain flour

25 g (1 oz) butter

2 onions, finely chopped

750 ml (1¼ pints) red wine

1 bay leaf

1 teaspoon thyme leaves

12 small onions, peeled

1 tablespoon cornflour

50 ml (2 fl oz) cold duck or chicken stock

1 teaspoon demerara sugar

salt and pepper

1 tablespoon parsley, chopped, to garnish

Prick the duckling pieces repeatedly with a fork. Place the flour on a plate, season with salt and pepper and coat the duckling with the mixture.

Melt the butter in a flameproof casserole, add the duckling pieces and cook for 10 minutes on each side until brown. Remove the duck and set aside.

Pour off all but 3 tablespoons of the fat in the casserole. Add the chopped onions and cook, stirring often, for 5 minutes. Return the duck to the casserole and stir in the wine, bay leaf and thyme and season with salt and pepper. Transfer the covered casserole to a preheated oven, 180°C (350°F), Gas Mark 4, and cook for 1 hour, turning the duck pieces occasionally.

Remove the casserole from the oven and stir in the small onions. Cover, return to the oven and continue cooking for 30 minutes.

Skim off any fat from the surface of the casserole and then transfer the duck pieces and onions to a heated serving platter. Keep warm.

Place the casserole over a medium heat and, using a whisk, combine the cornflour and stock in a cup until smooth, then pour into the casserole. Add the sugar. Stirring constantly, cook gently until the sauce has thickened. Adjust the seasoning, if necessary.

Arrange the duck pieces on a heated serving dish and place the small onions attractively around the duck. Coat with the sauce and sprinkle with chopped parsley.

Serves 2

left: casserole of duck with red cabbage
below: veal, mushroom and soured cream casserole

Veal, Mushroom and Soured Cream Casserole

40 g (1½ oz) butter
750 g (1½ lb) boneless veal, cut into
  2.5 cm (1 inch) cubes
1 onion, finely chopped
1 garlic clove, finely chopped
250 g (8 oz) field mushrooms, sliced
3 tablespoons plain flour
175 ml (6 fl oz) chicken stock
125 ml (4 fl oz) dry white wine
½ tablespoon thyme leaves
175 ml (6 fl oz) soured cream
salt and pepper
chives, to garnish

Melt the butter in a large pan and, when hot, add the veal. Stirring frequently, cook for about 5–10 minutes until browned on all sides. Remove and place in a casserole.

Add the onion, garlic and mushrooms and cook gently for 10 minutes. Sprinkle in the flour and cook, stirring, for 2–3 minutes. Blend in the stock, wine and thyme and cook for 2–3 minutes.

Season and remove from the heat. Allow to cool for 2 minutes. Blend the soured cream into the sauce and pour over the meat. Stir well. Cover and cook in a preheated oven, 150°C (300°F), Gas Mark 2, for 1½ hours. Garnish with chives and serve with buttered noodles.

Serves 4

45

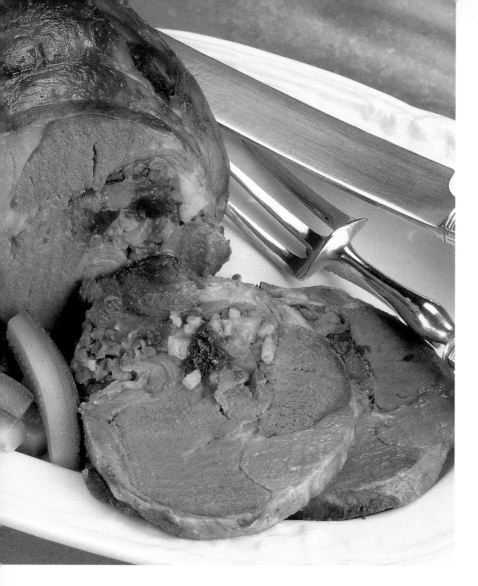

Pot Roast Colonial Lamb

1 x 2 kg (4 lb) leg of lamb, boned

Stuffing:

25 g (1 oz) butter or margarine

1 onion, finely chopped

2 celery sticks, finely chopped

3 rashers of bacon, derinded and chopped

75 g (3 oz) cooked rice

pinch of ground allspice

200 g (7 oz) can apricot halves

200 g (7 oz) can prunes

1 egg yolk

salt and pepper

Sauce:

150 ml (¼ pint) dry white wine

15 g (½ oz) melted butter

150 ml (¼ pint) beef stock

1½ tablespoons cornflour

To garnish:

courgettes, lightly cooked

rosemary or parsley sprigs, to garnish

For the stuffing, melt the fat in a pan and fry the onion, celery and bacon until lightly browned. Place in a bowl with the cooked rice and allspice and season with salt and pepper.

Drain the apricots and prunes, reserving the juices. Chop 4 apricots and 4 prunes and add them to the stuffing. Mix well and bind together with the egg yolk.

Use the stuffing to fill the boned cavity of the lamb, and skewer or sew loosely back into shape, using a trussing needle and fine string. Place the joint in a casserole with the wine, then cover and leave to marinate for several hours in a cool place, turning once.

Brush the surface of the meat with melted butter and sprinkle with salt. Cover and cook in the marinade in a preheated oven, 180°C (350°F), Gas Mark 4, for about 2¼ hours or until tender and cooked through. Baste the lamb once or twice during cooking and remove the casserole lid for the last 20–30 minutes to brown the joint.

Strain off the meat juices into a saucepan, remove any fat from the surface and add 150 ml (¼ pint) mixed reserved apricot and prune juice and the stock. Thicken with the cornflour blended with a little cold water and bring back to the boil for about 2 minutes. Serve the sauce separately in a sauceboat.

Remove the string or skewers from the lamb and place it on a serving dish. Garnish with the remaining apricots and prunes together with the courgettes and rosemary or parsley.

Serves 6

above: pot roast colonial lamb
right: steak, kidney and mushroom casserole

Steak, Kidney and Mushroom Casserole

750 g (1½ lb) stewing or braising
    steak, cut into 2 cm (¾ inch) cubes
125–175 g (4–6 oz) ox kidney,
    chopped
1 tablespoon plain flour
1 large onion, thinly sliced
300 ml (½ pint) beef stock
1–2 tablespoons tomato purée
600 ml (1 pint) water
1 teaspoon Worcestershire sauce
125 g (4 oz) mushrooms, sliced
salt and pepper
1 tablespoon parsley, chopped, to
    garnish

Put the steak and kidney in a bowl
with the flour and toss until well
coated, shaking off any excess flour.

Place the meat in a flameproof
casserole and add the onion, stock,
tomato purée and water and bring
to the boil. Add the Worcestershire
sauce and seasoning and then cover.

Place in a preheated oven, 160°C
(325°F), Gas Mark 3, and cook for
2 hours or until the meat is tender.
Add the mushrooms at this stage,
stirring them through the beef.
Return the casserole to the oven to
cook for a further 10–15 minutes.

Remove the casserole from the
oven and serve immediately,
garnished with the parsley.

Serves 4–6

Oxtail Casserole

2 tablespoons oil
2 oxtails, cut into 5 cm (2 inch) pieces
2 onions, sliced
1 garlic clove, crushed
2 tablespoons tomato purée
300 ml (½ pint) stock
150 ml (¼ pint) sherry
1 bouquet garni
500 g (1 lb) button onions, peeled
25 g (1 oz) butter
125 g (4 oz) butter mushrooms
salt and pepper

Heat the oil in a pan, then add the
oxtails and fry gently until lightly
browned. Remove to a casserole.

Add the onions and garlic to the
pan and sauté gently until golden.
Remove from the pan and arrange
on top of the oxtails.

Blend together the tomato purée,
stock and sherry and pour over the
contents of the casserole. Season
and add the bouquet garni. Cook in
a preheated oven, 160°C (325°F),
Gas Mark 3, for 2 hours or until the
meat comes away from the bones.

Remove the bouquet garni and
the meat from the casserole. Skim
the fat from the cooled sauce, then
return the meat to the casserole.

Sauté the onions in the butter for
10 minutes, add the mushrooms
and cook for a further 10 minutes,
then add both vegetables to the
meat. Simmer all the ingredients
together for 10 minutes, and adjust
the seasoning to taste before
serving. Serve with mashed potatoes
and a green vegetable.

Serves 4–6

Tex-mex Chilli

1 kg (2 lb) braising steak, trimmed
and cut into 2.5 cm (1 inch) cubes

5 tablespoons vegetable oil

4 tablespoons mild or medium-hot
chilli powder

3 onions, finely chopped

4 garlic cloves, finely chopped

1 tablespoon dried oregano

2 teaspoons ground cumin

2 x 425 g (14 oz) cans tomatoes,
drained and chopped

750 ml (1¼ pints) lager

175 g (6 oz) tomato purée

2 tablespoons red wine vinegar

2 x 425 g (14 oz) cans kidney beans,
drained

salt and pepper

Salsa:

3 large tomatoes, skinned, deseeded
and diced

50 ml (2 fl oz) lemon juice

25 ml (1 fl oz) lime juice

1 small onion, finely chopped

2 tablespoons fresh coriander, finely
chopped

1 large garlic clove, finely
chopped

2–4 green chillies, deseeded and
finely chopped

To serve:

250 ml (8 fl oz) soured cream

1 large avocado, stoned, peeled and
sliced

lime twists

125 g (4 oz) Cheddar cheese,
grated

8 spring onions, finely chopped

16–24 corn tortillas, heated

Coat the meat with 3 tablespoons of
the oil and 3 tablespoons of the
chilli powder. Cover and chill in the
refrigerator overnight.

Heat the remaining oil, add the
steak and then brown on all sides

for 5 minutes. Transfer the braising steak to a large flameproof casserole.

Add the onions to the pan and cook gently for 10 minutes until soft and golden. Stir in the garlic, remaining chilli powder, oregano and cumin and season with salt and pepper. Cook for 5 minutes, stirring occasionally. Remove from the heat and stir the onion mixture into the meat.

Stir the tomatoes, lager, tomato purée and vinegar into the meat mixture. Place the casserole over a medium-high heat and bring to the boil. Cover and cook in a preheated oven, 180°C (350°F), Gas Mark 4, for 3 hours, stirring occasionally. Stir the beans into the chilli and continue cooking, uncovered, for 30 minutes.

Make the salsa. Mix together the tomatoes, lemon and lime juice, onion, coriander, garlic and chillies in a bowl. Season with salt and pepper. Transfer to a serving dish and set aside.

Skim the fat from the casserole and simmer over a low heat until heated thoroughly. Taste and adjust the seasoning, if necessary.

Spoon onto 6 serving plates and serve with soured cream, slices of avocado, lime twists, the salsa, grated cheese, spring onions and tortillas.

Serves 6

Boeuf Bourguignon

175 ml (6 fl oz) dry, red Burgundy wine
125 ml (4 fl oz) cognac
1.5 kg (3 lb) braising steak, cubed
3 litres (5 pints) water
1 calf's foot, cut in half (optional)
50 g (2 oz) fresh pork rind
50 g (2 oz) butter
2 tablespoons plain flour
1.8 litres (3 pints) strong beef stock
1 bouquet garni
500 g (1 lb) mushrooms, quartered, stems removed and reserved
250 g (8 oz) bacon, derinded and cut into strips
24 small onions, peeled

Combine the red wine and cognac in a large shallow container. Add the beef, then toss well to coat all the pieces. Cover and marinate for 3 hours.

Bring 2.5 litres (4 pints) of water to the boil in a large pan. Add the calf's foot, if using, and cook for 10 minutes. Remove the foot and rinse under cold running water. Tie the foot in some muslin to retain its shape and set aside.

Return the water to the boil, add the pork rind and cook for 1 minute. Drain the rind and rinse under cold running water. Set aside.

Remove the meat from the marinade and pat dry with kitchen paper. Reserve the marinade. Melt 2 tablespoons of the butter in a large flameproof casserole, add the meat and brown on all sides. Remove the meat with a slotted spoon and set aside.

Using a whisk, stir the flour into the casserole. Cook for 2–3 minutes, stirring constantly. Gradually blend in the reserved marinade and stock. Bring to the boil, stirring until smooth. Return the meat to the casserole and add the bouquet garni, calf's foot, pork rind and the mushroom stems. Cover and cook in a preheated oven, 160°C (325°F), Gas Mark 3, for 2 hours.

While the casserole is cooking, bring the remaining water to the boil, add the bacon pieces and boil for 1 minute. Drain in a colander. Melt the remaining butter in a large frying pan and cook the bacon pieces for 10 minutes until well browned. Remove and drain on kitchen paper.

Add the onions to the frying pan and cook for 10–15 minutes until browned. Set aside.

Remove the casserole from the oven. Transfer the beef cubes to a heated platter. Remove the calf's foot and discard. Strain the sauce through a fine sieve and clean the casserole dish. Return the beef to the casserole. Add the bacon, onions, mushrooms and sauce. Bring to the boil over a medium heat. Cover and put back in the oven for 30 minutes, then serve.

Serves 6

Boeuf à la Mode

This classic dish can be served cold. Cut the meat into thin slices and arrange in a shallow dish. Arrange the carrots and onions around the slices. Pour over the sauce and chill overnight. If the sauce did not boil vigorously while cooking, it should set into a clear jelly.

250 g (8 oz) fresh pork fat, cut into
    20 cm (8 inch) long thin strips
⅛ teaspoon mixed spice
125 ml (4 fl oz) cognac
2 tablespoons parsley, chopped
1.75 kg (3½ lb) brisket, tied
2 tablespoons thyme leaves
1 bay leaf, crushed
1.2 litres (2 pints) dry white wine
3 litres (5 pints) water
2 calf's feet (or 4 pig's trotters), cut in
    half (optional)
50 g (2 oz) fresh pork rind
10 parsley sprigs
sprig of fresh thyme
1 bay leaf
6 tablespoons butter
1 carrot, quartered
1 onion, quartered
5 garlic cloves, peeled
2.5 litres (4 pints) veal or beef stock
salt and pepper
To garnish:
1 tablespoon butter
20 small onions, peeled
500 g (1 lb) carrots, cut into strips

Place the pork fat strips in a shallow container. Toss with the mixed spice, salt and pepper. Blend in 2 tablespoons of the cognac and

marinate for 20 minutes, turning the strips occasionally.

Sprinkle the pork fat strips with the parsley. With a larding needle, push the fat strips into the brisket in the direction of the grain of the meat. The strips should be evenly placed in the meat, forming a chequerboard pattern.

Season the brisket with thyme, the bay leaf, salt and pepper and place in a deep glass or ceramic bowl. Cover the meat with the white wine and remaining cognac. Cover and leave to marinate in the refrigerator for at least 5 hours, preferably overnight, turning the meat occasionally.

Put the water in a large saucepan. Add the calf's feet, if using, and bring to a boil. Boil for 10 minutes, then remove the saucepan from the heat. Remove the meat from the water with a slotted spoon, then rinse under cold running water. Tie the feet in a piece of muslin so they keep their shape and set aside.

Bring the water in the saucepan to the boil again. Add the pork rind and cook for 5 minutes. Transfer the rind to a colander and rinse under cold running water. Tie the rind in a piece of muslin and set aside.

Remove the meat from the marinade and wipe dry. Tie the parsley, thyme and bay leaf in a small square of muslin to make a bouquet garni.

Melt the butter in a flameproof casserole, add the meat, carrot and

onion and brown on all sides. Add the calf's feet, pork rind, bouquet garni and garlic, then stir in the marinade and stock. The meat should be completely covered. Bring just to the boil, skimming off any scum. Cover the casserole and cook in a preheated oven, 160°C (325°F), Gas Mark 3, for 2 hours.

Just before removing the casserole from the oven, make the vegetable garnish. Melt the butter in a large frying pan and brown the small onions on all sides.

Remove the casserole from the oven. Transfer the meat, the calf's feet and pork rind to a heated platter. Discard the carrot and onion. Cut the feet and rind into 1 cm (½ inch) square pieces. Strain the sauce through a fine sieve, then allow to sit for 5 minutes. Remove the fat from the top of the sauce and clean the casserole.

Return the meat, calf's feet, rind, onion and carrot garnish, and reserved stock to the cleaned casserole. Bring to the boil, then cover and cook for 1 hour in the preheated oven.

To serve, remove the string and slice the meat. Place it on a large heated serving platter. Surround with the calf's feet (if liked), rind, carrots and onions, Pour over just enough sauce to moisten. Serve the remaining sauce separately in a heated sauceboat.

Serves 6

Daube de Boeuf

1 kg (2 lb) best braising steak, cut into 5 cm (2 inch) pieces
1 garlic clove, crushed
1 tablespoon parsley, chopped
1 teaspoon dried thyme
4 tablespoons brandy
150 ml (¼ pint) dry white wine
3 tablespoons oil
2 carrots, sliced
2 onions, sliced
450 ml (¾ pint) beef stock
2–3 slices smoked cooked ham, diced
1 bay leaf
salt and pepper
chopped parsley, to garnish

Place the meat in a bowl. Add the garlic, parsley, thyme and brandy and mix well. Leave to stand for 15 minutes. Add the wine, then cover and leave to marinate for about 2 hours in a cool place, turning the meat at least once.

Drain the meat, reserving the marinade. Heat the oil in a pan and fry the meat to seal it all over, then place in a casserole.

Add the carrots and onions to the same fat and fry for 2 minutes. Add the marinade and stock and bring to the boil. Season with salt and pepper, then add the ham and bay leaf and pour into the casserole over the meat.

Cover tightly and then cook in a preheated oven, 150°C (300°F), Gas Mark 2, for about 3½ hours or until the beef is tender. Discard the bay leaf, adjust the seasoning if necessary and serve sprinkled with chopped parsley.

Serves 5–6

left: boeuf à la mode
above: daube de boeuf

New England Beef Dinner

1 x 1.5 kg (3 lb) salt brisket of beef
1 bouquet garni
1 teaspoon black peppercorns
4 cloves
1 onion, peeled
8 carrots, halved lengthways
8 small potatoes, halved
1 small, tight cabbage, quartered and
   cored
chopped parsley, to garnish

Put the brisket in a deep flameproof casserole, cover with cold water and then add the bouquet garni and peppercorns. Stick the cloves into the onion and add to the casserole. Cover and bring very slowly to the boil, skimming off any scum on the surface. Reduce the heat and then simmer very gently for 3 hours.

Add the carrots and potatoes, cover the casserole and continue simmering for 20 minutes. Stir in the cabbage and cook, covered, for a further 20–30 minutes or until the meat and vegetables are tender.

Lift out the meat onto a board, then slice it and arrange the slices on a heated serving dish. Surround with the drained vegetables. Strain the broth, taste and adjust the seasoning, if necessary, and pour a little over the meat; serve the remainder separately.

Sprinkle with chopped parsley and serve immediately with plenty of fresh crusty bread.

Serves 6–8

Osso Bucco

25 g (1 oz) butter
2 tablespoons olive oil
1 kg (2 lb) shin of veal, cut into
   4 equal pieces
1 onion, thinly sliced
500 g (1 lb) tomatoes, skinned and
   sliced
1 garlic clove, crushed
150 ml (¼ pint) dry white wine
150 ml (¼ pint) veal or chicken stock
1 bay leaf
salt and pepper
Gremolata:
2 tablespoons parsley, chopped
1 garlic clove, finely chopped
grated rind of 1 small lemon

Melt the butter with the oil in a flameproof casserole, add the veal and brown on all sides. Remove the veal and keep warm.

Add the onion to the casserole and cook gently until soft and golden. Stir in the tomatoes, garlic and white wine. Allow to bubble for a few minutes, then return the meat to the casserole with the stock and bay leaf. Season with salt and pepper. Cover and simmer gently for 2 hours or until the meat is really tender and the sauce is rich and thick.

Meanwhile, mix together the parsley, garlic and lemon rind for the gremolata.

Serve the veal sprinkled with the gremolata. A traditional accompaniment is a bowl of risotto milanese (rice which has been cooked slowly with white wine, saffron and beef marrow).

Serves 4

Paupiettes de Veau

8 x 50 g (2 oz) veal escalopes
125 g (4 oz) Parma ham, cut to fit the escalopes
8 fresh sage leaves
1 tablespoon butter
1 tablespoon oil
salt and pepper
sprigs of watercress, to garnish
Madeira sauce:
250 g (8 oz) bacon, rinded and cut into strips

15 g (½ oz) butter
3 large tomatoes, skinned, deseeded and diced
2 carrots, sliced
1 large onion, sliced
4 tablespoons plain flour
750 ml (1¼ pints) strong beef stock
125 ml (4 fl oz) Madeira wine
1 tablespoon thyme leaves
1 bay leaf, crushed

For the sauce, put the bacon pieces in a large saucepan over a moderate heat. Cook, stirring frequently, for 10 minutes until crisp. Remove the bacon and drain on kitchen paper. Set aside.

Melt the butter in the saucepan and add the tomatoes, carrots and onion. Cook for 10 minutes until the onion is soft and golden. Blend in the flour, stirring constantly, and then cook for 2–3 minutes. Using a whisk, gradually stir in the stock and Madeira. Bring to the boil, stirring constantly, then simmer for 5 minutes until smooth and thick. Add the thyme and bay leaf, and season with salt and pepper.

Remove from the heat and stir in the bacon pieces. Set aside.

Take the veal escalopes and place 1 slice of Parma ham on each. Top with the sage leaves and roll up the escalopes, securing with metal skewers or wooden cocktail sticks. Season each escalope with salt and pepper and set aside.

Heat the butter and oil in a large flameproof casserole. Add the escalopes and brown on all sides for 5 minutes, turning occasionally. Drain off the excess fat and discard.

Coat the veal escalopes with the sauce, then cover and cook in a preheated oven, 180°C (350°F), Gas Mark 4, for 45 minutes. Serve the escalopes on a heated platter with the sauce poured over them. Serve immediately, garnished with sprigs of watercress.

Serves 6

left: New England beef dinner
below: paupiettes de veau

Pork Rib Casserole with Chilli Biscuits

1.5 kg (3 lb) lean pork spareribs
3 tablespoons vegetable oil
1 large onion, finely chopped
4 garlic cloves, finely chopped
2 x 425 g (14 oz) cans tomatoes
475 ml (16 fl oz) beef stock
75 ml (3 fl oz) cider vinegar
50 g (2 oz) demerara sugar
3 tablespoons Worcestershire sauce
2 tablespoons Dijon mustard
2 tablespoons lemon juice
1 teaspoon parsley, chopped
½ teaspoon paprika
½ teaspoon ground cayenne pepper
salt and pepper
Chilli biscuits:
15 g (½ oz) butter
1 onion, finely chopped
1 garlic clove, finely chopped
375 g (12 oz) plain flour
1 tablespoon baking powder
2 teaspoons mild chilli powder
50 g (2 oz) Parmesan cheese, freshly grated
2 tablespoons fresh coriander, finely chopped
50 g (2 oz) well-chilled lard, cubed
175 ml (6 fl oz) milk

Arrange the ribs in a single layer in a large, shallow roasting pan. Grill under a preheated hot grill, turning frequently, until brown.

Heat the oil in a large flameproof casserole and add the onion and garlic. Cook gently for 10 minutes until softened. Stir in the tomatoes, stock, vinegar, sugar, Worcestershire sauce, mustard, lemon juice, parsley and spices. Add the ribs and season with salt and pepper. Cover and cook in a preheated oven, 190°C (375°F), Gas Mark 5 for 1¾ hours until the ribs are tender.

For the biscuits, melt the butter in a frying pan and add the onion and garlic. Cook gently for about 10 minutes over a low heat until softened. Cool for 10 minutes.

Sift the flour, baking powder, chilli powder and salt into a bowl. Stir in the cheese and coriander. Cut in the chilled lard until the mixture resembles coarse crumbs, and blend in the onion mixture. Make a well in the centre of the flour mixture, pour in the milk and then mix with a fork until a dough is formed.

Turn out on to a lightly floured surface and knead 5 times. Roll the dough out, 1 cm (½ inch) thick. Using a 7.5 cm (3 inch) floured cutter, cut out 6–8 biscuits and then place them on a baking sheet.

When the ribs have cooked for 1¾ hours, uncover the casserole and increase the oven temperature to

230°C (450°F), Gas Mark 8. Bake the biscuits for 12–15 minutes until they are puffed up and lightly browned. Arrange the biscuits around the ribs and serve immediately.

Serves 6

Pork Medley

12 pork medallions, about 2.5 cm
  (1 inch) thick
300 ml (½ pint) dry cider
4 tablespoons plain flour
2 tablespoons vegetable oil
250 g (8 oz) button mushrooms,
  halved
1 large onion, chopped
1 green pepper, cored, deseeded and
  chopped
2 tomatoes, cored and quartered
1 garlic clove, finely chopped
salt and pepper
4 sprigs of parsley, to garnish
Sauce:
40 g (1½ oz) butter
3 tablespoons plain flour
250 ml (8 fl oz) beef stock
1 tablespoon fresh thyme
125 ml (4 fl oz) double cream

Put the pork and cider in a large, shallow dish. Cover and chill in the refrigerator overnight.

Remove the pork from the cider and pat dry with kitchen paper. Reserve the cider to make the sauce. Place 2 tablespoons of the flour on a large plate and season with the salt and pepper. Toss the pork medallions in the flour mixture, coating well.

Heat the oil in a large frying pan and when the pan is hot, but not smoking, add the pork. Cook for 2–3 minutes, shaking the pan frequently to prevent sticking, until the medallions are browned. Turn over and continue cooking for about 2–3 minutes. Remove the pork from the pan and place in a large flameproof casserole. Surround with the mushrooms, onion, green pepper, tomatoes and garlic.

For the sauce, melt the butter over a moderate heat and blend in the flour. Cook for 2–3 minutes, stirring frequently. Using a whisk, gradually add the stock and bring the mixture to a simmer, stirring continuously. Cook for 2–3 minutes until the sauce is thick and smooth. Blend in the reserved cider and add the thyme. Pour the sauce over the pork and vegetables.

Cook, covered, in a preheated oven, 180°C (350°F), Gas Mark 4, for 45 minutes or until the pork is cooked and tender.

Transfer the pork medallions to a heated serving platter. Remove the vegetables and arrange them around the medallions.

Heat the sauce in the casserole dish over a high heat. Stir in the cream, then taste and correct the seasoning, if necessary. Pour the sauce over the pork medallions and garnish with the parsley sprigs. Serve immediately.

Serves 6

left: pork rib casserole with chilli biscuits
above: *pork medley*

Braised Stuffed Shoulder of Lamb

The lamb shoulder must be boned. When it is boned, you will find that there is a pocket in the centre of the shoulder. Cut the pocket to extend it almost, but not through, the shoulder. One end of the shoulder should still be intact. The stuffing can then be placed in the pocket.

2 garlic cloves, cut into slivers
1 x 1.5 kg (3 lb) shoulder of lamb, boned, pocket cut and bones reserved
1 tablespoon rosemary, chopped
3 tablespoons vegetable oil
475 ml (16 fl oz) lamb or beef stock
50 g (2 oz) onion, diced
50 g (2 oz) carrot, diced
25 g (1 oz) celery, diced
150 g (5 oz) potatoes, diced
2 tablespoons cornflour
50 ml (2 fl oz) port
50 ml (2 fl oz) lamb or beef stock
salt and pepper
sprigs of mint, to garnish

Stuffing:
50 g (2 oz) butter
1 small onion, finely chopped
75 g (3 oz) mushrooms, sliced
125 g (4 oz) crustless day-old white bread, diced
75 g (3 oz) pine nuts
25 g (1 oz) chopped parsley
2 celery sticks, finely chopped
2 eggs, beaten
1 tablespoon tarragon, chopped
1 tablespoon mint, chopped
½ teaspoon paprika

For the stuffing, melt the butter and cook the onion and mushrooms for 10 minutes, stirring frequently. Remove from the heat and tip into a large bowl. Add the remaining stuffing ingredients and stir gently until well combined.

Insert the slivers of garlic under the skin of the lamb. Lay the lamb out flat, skin-side down. Place the stuffing evenly in the pocket of the shoulder. Close the open end of the shoulder with 4 metal skewers. Roll the meat to tuck the long ends of the lamb underneath and then tie firmly with string. Sprinkle the lamb with the rosemary and a little salt and pepper.

Heat the oil in a large frying pan and place the stuffed lamb in the pan. Brown on all sides, using 2 large spoons to turn the joint. Remove the lamb from the pan and set aside.

Pour 250 ml (8 fl oz) of the stock into a large casserole. Add the lamb and the reserved bones. Cover and cook in a preheated oven, 160°C (325°F), Gas Mark 3, for 45 minutes.

Remove the casserole from the oven, then add the remaining stock, onion, carrot, celery and potatoes. Cover and return to the oven for 1 hour. Transfer the cooked lamb and vegetables to a heated platter and keep warm. Discard the bones and skim off the fat from the sauce.

Bring the sauce to the boil in a large saucepan. In a bowl, thoroughly combine the cornflour, port and stock and then whisk it into the sauce. Cook for 4–5 minutes, stirring constantly, until thick and smooth. Strain the sauce into a heated sauceboat.

Place the lamb on a heated serving platter and garnish with mint. Serve the sauce separately. Serve with boiled new potatoes and vegetables, such as mangetout or baby sweetcorn.

Serves 6

Lamb Shrewsbury

50 g (2 oz) plain flour
1 tablespoon rosemary, finely
   chopped
6 x 175 g (6 oz) loin lamb chops
50 g (2 oz) butter
1 onion, finely chopped
1 carrot, sliced
1 large tomato, skinned, deseeded
   and diced
1 garlic clove, finely chopped
2 tablespoons tomato purée
125 ml (4 fl oz) port wine
900 ml (1½ pints) beef stock
4 tablespoons redcurrant jelly
salt and pepper
sprigs of watercress, to garnish

Mix together the flour and rosemary and season with salt and pepper. Coat the chops in this mixture.

Heat the butter in a flameproof casserole, add the chops and brown on one side for 5 minutes. Turn the chops over and cook on the other side for 5 minutes. Add the onion, carrot, tomato and garlic and blend in the tomato purée, port, stock and redcurrant jelly.

Cover the casserole and cook in a preheated oven, 180°C (350°F), Gas Mark 4, for 1 hour. Remove the chops from the sauce and place on a heated serving platter.

Strain the sauce and return to the casserole. Simmer for 10 minutes over a moderate heat until thick. Pour the sauce over the chops and serve garnished with watercress.

Serves 6

far left: braised stuffed shoulder of lamb
left: lamb Shrewsbury

Brittany Fish Casserole

This fish stew can be prepared in advance and then reheated within 15 minutes, so you can impress your guests with the appearance of little effort.

4 tablespoons lemon juice

2 tablespoons chives, finely chopped

1 tablespoon parsley, finely chopped

1 tablespoon tarragon, finely chopped

500 g (1 lb) skinned and boned salmon steaks, cut into 2.5 cm (1 inch) cubes

500 g (1 lb) skinned and boned halibut steaks, cut into 2.5 cm (1 inch) cubes

500 g (1 lb) thick sole fillets, cut into 1 cm (½ inch) strips

500 g (1 lb) small scallops

250 g (8 oz) large raw prawns, peeled and deveined

500 g (1 lb) mussels, scrubbed and debearded

2 shallots, finely chopped

250 ml (8 fl oz) water

125 g (4 oz) cauliflower florets

125 g (4 oz) broccoli florets

Fish base:

1.75 kg (4 lb) fish bones, rinsed and broken into small pieces

4.75 litres (8 pints) water

450 ml (¾ pint) fish stock

300 ml (½ pint) dry white wine

4 onions, sliced

1 carrot, sliced

12 sprigs of parsley

1 bay leaf

1 tablespoon thyme leaves, chopped

To finish:

8 tablespoons cornflour

350 ml (12 fl oz) double or whipping cream

1 tablespoon parsley, finely chopped

salt and pepper

To make the fish base, put the fish bones, water, stock, 250 ml (8 fl oz) of the wine, onions, carrot, parsley, bay leaf and thyme in a large pan. Bring to the boil, then reduce the heat and simmer for 45 minutes. Crush the bones occasionally with a wooden spoon while simmering.

Ladle the mixture through a strainer lined with several layers of dampened muslin and strain into a large saucepan. Cover and set aside.

Blend together the lemon juice, chives, parsley and tarragon in a small bowl. Combine the salmon, halibut, sole, scallops and prawns in a large shallow pan. Pour the lemon juice mixture over the fish and toss gently to coat. Cover and chill in the refrigerator.

Put the mussels, remaining white wine and shallots into a saucepan. Cover and cook over a medium-high heat for 3–4 minutes. Using a slotted spoon, remove any opened mussels to a large bowl. Cover and continue cooking the remaining mussels for 2 minutes. Transfer the remaining opened mussels to the bowl and be careful to discard any mussels that do not open. Reserve the cooking liquid.

Remove the mussels from their shells, discarding the shells. Cover and set aside. Ladle the cooking liquid into the fish base through a

1 tablespoon Worcestershire sauce

425 g (14 oz) can tomatoes

300 ml (½ pint) tomato juice

125 g (4 oz) long-grain rice

125 g (4 oz) okra, stems removed, sliced

250 g (8 oz) cooked peeled prawns, fresh or frozen

250 g (8 oz) dressed crabmeat, fresh or frozen

4 tablespoons dry sherry

salt and pepper

To garnish:

garlic croûtons

parsley, chopped

strainer lined with several layers of muslin. Cover and set aside.

Bring the water to the boil in a saucepan. Add the cauliflower and cook for 3–4 minutes until tender but still crisp. Remove with a slotted spoon and place in a colander under cold running water. When the cauliflower is cool, drain well, then cover and set aside.

Add the broccoli florets to the pan of boiling water and cook for 2–3 minutes until just tender. Remove with a slotted spoon and place in a colander under cold running water. When the broccoli is cool, drain, cover and set aside.

Ladle the vegetable liquid into the fish base through a strainer lined with several layers of muslin. Cover and set aside.

To finish the casserole, drain the marinated fish and shellfish. Place in a large flameproof casserole. Bring the fish base to a boil. Put the cornflour in a bowl and gradually blend in the cream until smooth.

Whisk the cornflour mixture into the fish base and, stirring constantly, cook for 5 minutes over a low heat until the sauce is smooth and thick.

Pour the fish base into the casserole. Place the casserole over a medium-high heat and then cook for 5 minutes. Add the mussels, cauliflower, broccoli and chopped parsley, then heat through. Season with salt and pepper and serve immediately.

Serves 8

Prawn Gumbo with Rice

2 tablespoons oil

2 celery sticks, finely sliced

1 onion, diced

1 green pepper, cored, deseeded and diced

1 garlic clove, crushed

Heat the oil in a large flameproof casserole and cook the celery, onion and pepper gently for 5 minutes. Add the garlic, Worcestershire sauce, tomatoes and tomato juice, and season with salt and pepper.

Stir in the rice and okra, and bring gently to simmering point. Cover and then cook in a preheated oven, 160°C (325°F), Gas Mark 3, for 1 hour.

Gently stir in the prawns, crabmeat and sherry; if the rice looks a little dry, add some more tomato juice. Re-cover, and return to the oven for 15 minutes. Pour into a heated serving dish, arrange the croûtons at either end and sprinkle with chopped parsley.

Serves 8

left: Brittany fish casserole
above: prawn gumbo with rice

New England Oysters

This recipe breaks two rules about oysters. Purists will object to cooking oysters. They maintain that an oyster is best when eaten raw – and heaven forbid that you should add salt, cocktail sauce or vinegar to these freshly shelled morsels! The second broken rule is the peculiarity of adding cracker crumbs to this recipe. In fact, scalloped oysters were a virtual institution in England and North America in the 1800s when a glut of oysters tested cooks' ingenuity – hence the evolution of this dish.

500 g (1 lb) freshly shelled oysters, with 125 ml (4 fl oz) of the oyster liquor reserved
125 ml (4 fl oz) double or whipping cream
40 g (1½ oz) melted butter
125 g (4 oz) salted cracker crumbs
shake of Tabasco sauce
pepper

Place a sieve lined with a double thickness of muslin over a bowl. Drain the oyster liquor in the sieve and reserve. Remove any pieces of shell or grit from the oysters. Rinse briefly, then drain well in the sieve. Combine the reserved oyster liquor with the cream and set aside.

Grease a large casserole dish with 1 tablespoon of the melted butter. Place one-third of the crumbs on the bottom of the dish. Arrange half of the drained oysters over the crumbs and season lightly with pepper and Tabasco sauce. Pour half of the oyster liquor mixture over the oysters. Top evenly with another third of the crumbs and arrange the remaining oysters over the crumbs. Season with pepper and Tabasco sauce. Pour the remaining oyster liquor over the oysters, top with the remaining crumbs and dot with the remaining butter.

Cook the casserole, uncovered, in a preheated oven, 200°C (400°F), Gas Mark 6, for 30 minutes until the cream is bubbling and the crumbs are golden brown.

Serves 3–4

Avocado Seafood Casserole

125 g (4 oz) butter
1 large ripe avocado, halved, stoned, peeled and cubed
2 teaspoons lemon juice
375 g (12 oz) cooked white crabmeat
375 g (12 oz) cooked peeled prawns
375 g (12 oz) cooked scallops, halved if large
175 g (6 oz) onion, finely chopped
125 g (4 oz) plain flour
425 ml (14 fl oz) single cream
425 ml (14 fl oz) milk
1 teaspoon Dijon mustard
175 g (6 oz) Gruyère cheese, grated
1 tablespoon thyme leaves
salt and pepper
To garnish:
½ avocado, halved, stoned, peeled and cut into a fan shape
1 sprig of parsley (optional)

Grease a 23 x 33 cm (9 x 13 inch) casserole dish with 15 g (½ oz) of the butter. Set aside. Toss the avocado with the lemon juice in a bowl, and then combine the avocado with the crabmeat, prawns and scallops in the casserole.

Melt the remaining butter in a large saucepan and cook the onion, stirring frequently, for 10 minutes until soft and golden. Lower the heat and then blend in the flour. Stirring constantly, cook gently for 2–3 minutes. Using a whisk, gradually add the cream, milk and mustard. Increase the heat to medium and cook for 5 minutes, stirring constantly, until the sauce is smooth and thick.

Stir the cheese into the sauce. Remove the saucepan from the heat and add the thyme. Season with salt and pepper. Gently blend the sauce into the seafood mixture.

Bake the casserole in a preheated oven, 180°C (350°F), Gas Mark 4, for 30–40 minutes until heated through. Garnish with the avocado fan and parsley, if liked. Serve with rice and a tomato salad.

Serves 8

Scallop Casserole

1.5 kg (3 lb) freshly shelled scallops with corals
⅛ teaspoon saffron threads
250 ml (8 fl oz) white vermouth
250 ml (8 fl oz) double or whipping cream
¼ teaspoon lemon juice
1 tablespoon chervil, finely chopped
1 tablespoon chives, snipped
Court bouillon:
8 small onions, peeled
4 carrots, sliced
3 celery sticks, sliced
1 leek, white part only, chopped
12 sprigs of parsley

1 bay leaf
1 sprig of thyme
1 sprig of tarragon
⅛ teaspoon ground coriander
⅛ teaspoon saffron threads
1 clove
pinch of cayenne pepper
2.5 litres (4 pints) water
salt and pepper

Put all the ingredients for the court bouillon in a large saucepan. Cover the pan and bring to the boil. Boil for 10 minutes, then remove from the heat and set aside until cool.

Place the scallops in one layer in a large flameproof casserole. Heat the court bouillon until just boiling and strain over the scallops. Cook gently over a medium-low heat for 4 minutes.

Remove from the heat and then strain the court bouillon into a large saucepan and reserve. Cover the scallops and keep warm.

Boil the court bouillon over a high heat until reduced to 250 ml (8 fl oz). Remove 25 ml (1 fl oz) and soak the saffron threads in this.

Add the vermouth and cream to the court bouillon. Return the sauce to the boil. Add the lemon juice and saffron mixture and then stir in the chervil and chives. Pour the sauce over the scallops, then cover and stand for 5 minutes before serving.

Serves 6

left: avocado seafood casserole
above: New England oysters

Exotic Dishes

Polynesian Poussins

3 tablespoons oil
4 x 450 g (1 lb) poussins
500 g (1 lb) can pineapple chunks in syrup
chicken stock, for mixing
2 teaspoons cornflour
1 tablespoon tomato purée
1 onion, sliced
1 red pepper, cored, deseeded and sliced
50 g (2 oz) macadamia nuts, chopped
salt and pepper
sprig of parsley, to garnish

Heat the oil in a frying pan and brown the poussins on all sides, then transfer them to a casserole, reserving the oil in the frying pan.

Drain off the syrup from the pineapple and make up to 300 ml (½ pint) with chicken stock. Mix a little of this liquid with the cornflour and tomato purée and put all the liquid into a small saucepan. Bring to the boil and then pour over the poussins.

Cover the casserole and cook in a preheated oven, 190°C (375°F), Gas Mark 5, for 1–1¼ hours until the poussins are tender, basting them occasionally.

When the poussins are cooked, heat the reserved oil in the frying pan and lightly fry the onion and red pepper until soft. Strain the liquid from the casserole into the frying pan, add the pineapple and salt and pepper to taste, and boil until the mixture becomes syrupy.

Put the poussins on a warmed serving dish, pour the sauce over and sprinkle with the macadamia nuts. Serve at once.

Serves 4

Nigerian Chicken and Peanut Casserole

This recipe is best made with a standard peanut butter containing an emulsifier. If a peanut butter without an emulsifier is used, 1 teaspoon of cornflour should be added to the stock with the peanut butter to prevent the oil in it separating.

2 tablespoons oil
1 large onion, chopped
½ teaspoon chilli powder
1 teaspoon ground cumin
300 ml (½ pint) chicken stock
125 g (4 oz) crunchy peanut butter
4 chicken joints, about 375 g (12 oz) each

250 g (8 oz) tomatoes, skinned,
    deseeded and chopped
salt and pepper
To garnish:
chilli powder
parsley, finely chopped

Heat the oil in a pan, add the onion
and fry gently until soft. Add the
chilli and cumin to the pan and
cook for 1 minute. Add the stock
and peanut butter. Season with salt
and pepper and bring to the boil,
stirring well.

Skin the chicken joints and place
in a casserole. Add the tomatoes
and cover with the peanut sauce.
Cover the casserole and cook in a
preheated oven, 180°C (350°F), Gas
Mark 4, for 1–1¼ hours until the
chicken is very tender, turning the
chicken from time to time.

Garnish with a little chilli powder
and the finely chopped parsley.

Serves 4

Moroccan Chicken with Saffron, Lemon and Olives

4 boned chicken breasts with skin,
    about 175 g (6 oz) each
2 tablespoons clear honey
15 g (½ oz) butter
75 ml (3 fl oz) chicken stock

pinch of saffron
½ teaspoon ground ginger
½ teaspoon ground turmeric
2 tablespoons lemon juice
125 g (4 oz) green olives, pitted
salt and pepper
To garnish:
4 lemon wedges
fresh chives

Brush the chicken skin with a little
of the honey. Melt the butter in a
frying pan, put the chicken in, skin-
side down, and cook gently until
the skin is a rich brown colour,
taking care not to burn it. Transfer
the chicken, skin-side up, to a
shallow casserole dish.

Pour the stock, remaining honey,
saffron, ginger, turmeric and lemon
juice into the pan, season with salt
and pepper, bring to the boil and
then pour around the chicken
breasts in the casserole. The liquid
should not cover the skin.

Cook, uncovered, in a preheated
oven, 200°C (400°F), Gas Mark 6,
for 40 minutes. Add the olives to
the casserole and cook for a further
5 minutes. Serve garnished with the
lemon wedges and chives.

Serves 4

above: Polynesian poussins
*left: Moroccan chicken with
saffron, lemon and olives*

Mughlai Chicken

25 g (1 oz) butter
1 tablespoon oil
500 g (1 lb) onions, chopped
1 garlic clove, crushed
1 teaspoon ground coriander
½ teaspoon ground ginger
pinch of ground cloves
1 teaspoon chilli powder
1 teaspoon cardamom seeds
2 teaspoons ground cumin
1 teaspoon ground turmeric
150 ml (5 fl oz) double or whipping
  cream
150 ml (5 fl oz) natural yogurt
1 x 1.5 kg (3 lb) chicken
salt and pepper

To garnish:
sprigs of fresh coriander
raw onion rings

Melt the butter and oil together in a pan, add the onions and garlic and cook until softened. Mix the spices together and add to the pan. Cook for 1–2 minutes.

Put the cream and yogurt into a blender or food processor. Add the onion and spice mixture, season with salt and pepper, and then blend to a smooth purée.

Skin the chicken and place in a casserole. Pour the puréed spicy yogurt mixture over the chicken. Cover the casserole and cook in a preheated oven, 190°C (375°F), Gas Mark 5, for 1½ hours, basting the chicken from time to time.

Remove the casserole from the oven, then transfer the chicken to a heated serving dish and pour the sauce over. Garnish with fresh coriander and onion rings.

Serves 4

above: mughlai chicken
right: Mexican chicken in green almond sauce

Mexican Chicken in Green Almond Sauce

4 chicken joints, about 375 g (12 oz)
  each
1 onion, chopped
1 garlic clove, crushed
1 green chilli, deseeded
300 ml (½ pint) hot chicken stock
large bunch of parsley, stalks removed
large bunch of fresh coriander, stalks
  removed
50 g (2 oz) ground almonds
25 g (1 oz) flaked almonds
salt and pepper
watercress and cherry tomatoes, to
  serve (optional)

Skin the chicken joints and put
them in an even layer in a casserole.

Add the onion, garlic, green chilli,
season with salt and pepper and
pour the stock over. Cover the
casserole and cook in a preheated
oven, 180°C (350°F), Gas Mark 4,
for 1–1¼ hours until the chicken is
cooked.

Remove the casserole from the
oven. Put the stock, onion, garlic
and chilli into a blender or food
processor, and then add the parsley,
coriander and ground almonds.
Blend to a thick sauce. Taste and
adjust the seasoning, if necessary.

Sprinkle the flaked almonds over
the chicken and pour the sauce
over. Cover the casserole and return
to the oven for a further 15 minutes
to heat through. Serve hot with a
watercress and cherry tomato salad,
if liked.

Serves 4

Chinese Five-spice Chicken Legs

Five-spice powder is available from most
supermarkets as well as from Chinese
food stores and delicatessens.

1 tablespoon sesame oil
8 chicken drumsticks, skinned
1 small bunch of spring onions, sliced
250 g (8 oz) can bamboo shoots,
  drained
2 teaspoons cornflour
2 tablespoons soy sauce
3 tablespoons dry sherry
75 ml (3 fl oz) water
2 teaspoons five-spice powder
salt and pepper

Heat the oil in a pan and lightly fry
the chicken drumsticks. Transfer
them to a casserole, and then add
the spring onions, reserving about
1 tablespoon for the garnish, and
the bamboo shoots.

Mix the cornflour with the soy
sauce, sherry, water and five-spice
powder, and then add to the oil
remaining in the pan. Bring to the
boil, taste and adjust the seasoning.
Pour over the chicken drumsticks.

Cover the casserole and cook in a
preheated oven, 180°C (350°F), Gas
Mark 4, for 1 hour. Serve garnished
with the reserved spring onions.

Serves 4

Turkey Mole

15 g (1 oz) lard
750 g (1½ lb) boneless turkey breast, diced
1 onion, chopped
1 garlic clove, crushed
300 ml (½ pint) chicken stock
1 green chilli, deseeded and chopped
2 green peppers, cored, deseeded and chopped
2 tomatoes, skinned, deseeded and chopped
50 g (2 oz) blanched almonds
50 g (2 oz) raisins
1 teaspoon ground coriander
½ teaspoon ground anise or aniseed
pinch of ground cloves
½ teaspoon ground cinnamon
¼ teaspoon dried red pepper flakes
25 g (1 oz) plain chocolate, broken into pieces
salt and pepper

Melt the lard in a frying pan and fry the turkey in batches until brown. Transfer it with a slotted spoon to a casserole. Add the onion and garlic to the pan and cook until soft.

In a blender or food processor, put the chicken stock, chilli, green pepper, tomatoes, almonds, raisins, spices and red pepper flakes and blend until smooth.

Pour into the frying pan, add the chocolate and salt and pepper, and

Duck Fesanjan

3 pomegranates
chicken stock, to mix
1 tablespoon oil
4 boneless duck breasts, about 175 g (6 oz) each, skinned
1 small onion, chopped
2 teaspoons lemon juice
½ teaspoon ground cinnamon
pinch of chilli powder
1 tablespoon clear honey
salt and pepper
To garnish:
seeds of 1 pomegranate
25 g (1 oz) walnuts, chopped

Cut the pomegranates in half, put the seeds into a sieve and push through to extract the juice. Discard the pips and make the pomegranate juice up to 300 ml (½ pint) with the chicken stock.

Heat the oil in a frying pan. Fry the duck for 1 minute on each side, then transfer to a shallow casserole.

Add the onion to the pan and cook for 1 minute. Add the pomegranate juice, lemon juice, cinnamon, chilli powder and honey to the pan and season with salt and pepper. Bring to the boil and pour over the duck.

Cover the casserole and put into a preheated oven, 180°C (350°F), Gas Mark 4. Cook for 40–50 minutes until the duck is tender. Take the duck breasts out of the casserole with a slotted spoon, place on a serving dish and keep warm.

Pour the juices from the casserole into a small saucepan and boil until reduced by half. Pour over the duck and sprinkle with the pomegranate seeds and chopped walnuts.

Serves 4

above: duck fesanjan
above right: turkey mole
right: spicy braised duck

stir until the chocolate has melted. Bring to the boil and then simmer for 5 minutes. Pour over the turkey and mix well.

Cover the casserole, put into a preheated oven, 180°C (350°F), Gas Mark 4, and cook for 1 hour. Serve immediately with some rice.

Serves 4–6

Spicy Braised Duck

1 x 2.5 kg (5 lb) duck, jointed
small piece of cinnamon stick
1 star anise
1 teaspoon whole cardamoms
1 tablespoon oil
1 onion, chopped
2 garlic cloves, crushed
1 tablespoon fresh root ginger, grated
2 tablespoons soy sauce
1 tablespoon soft brown sugar
300 ml (½ pint) chicken stock

salt and pepper
spring onion fans, to garnish (optional)

Remove the skin and any excess fat and bones from the duck joints, and then put them into a large casserole with the cinnamon, star anise and cardamoms.

Heat the oil in a saucepan, add the onion, garlic and ginger and cook for 2–3 minutes. Add the soy sauce, brown sugar and chicken stock to the pan and season with salt and pepper. Bring to the boil and then pour over the duck and cover the casserole.

Cook in a preheated oven, 160°C (325°F), Gas Mark 3, for 1½–2 hours, turning the duck from time to time, until the duck is quite tender. When the duck is cooked, take it out of the casserole with a slotted spoon. Transfer to a warm serving dish and keep warm.

Pour the liquid through a sieve into a clean saucepan, discarding the cinnamon, star anise and cardamoms. Push the onion, garlic and ginger through the sieve and reheat the sauce, reducing it a little, if necessary, to achieve a coating consistency. Pour over the duck and then serve, garnished with the spring onion fans, if using.

Serves 4

Chilli Con Carne

175 g (6 oz) pinto beans, soaked
    overnight
2 tablespoons oil
500 g (1 lb) chuck steak, finely diced
1 onion, chopped
1 green chilli, deseeded and finely
    chopped
1 teaspoon dried oregano
1 tablespoon ground cumin
½ teaspoon dried red pepper flakes
425 g (14 oz) can chopped tomatoes
300 ml (½ pint) beef stock
salt and pepper

Put the beans into a pan of cold water, bring to the boil and boil rapidly for 10 minutes, then drain.

Heat the oil in a flameproof casserole, add the chuck steak and cook, turning frequently, until browned all over. Add the onion and chilli and cook for 2–3 minutes. Add the oregano, cumin, pepper flakes, tomatoes and juice, stock and beans to the casserole and bring to the boil.

Cover and cook in a preheated oven, 160°C (325°F), Gas Mark 3, for 1½ hours until the beef and beans are tender. Taste and adjust the seasoning, if necessary, before serving.

Serves 4

Argentine Beef Peaches

When fresh peaches are not available, a 500 g (1 lb) can of peaches in natural juice can be used.

2 tablespoons oil
500 g (1 lb) chuck steak, diced
1 large onion, chopped
1 garlic clove, crushed
1 tablespoon plain flour
300 ml (½ pint) beef stock
150 ml (¼ pint) red wine
1 tablespoon tomato purée
1 teaspoon dried oregano
500 g (1 lb) sweet potatoes, diced
3 ripe peaches, skinned and sliced
250 g (8 oz) whole baby sweetcorn or
    500 g (1 lb) can, drained
salt and pepper

Heat the oil in a large flameproof casserole and fry the beef until browned, then add the onion and garlic and cook for 2–3 minutes. Add the flour to the pan and cook for a further minute.

Pour in the stock and red wine, and then add the tomato purée, oregano and sweet potatoes. Season with salt and pepper and bring to the boil.

Cover the casserole, put into a preheated oven, 180°C (350°F), Gas Mark 4, and cook for 1 hour. Add the peaches and sweetcorn to the casserole and then cook for a further 15 minutes.

Serves 4

Sauerbraten

75 ml (3 fl oz) red wine
75 ml (3 fl oz) red wine vinegar
1 bay leaf
1 teaspoon dried marjoram
1 teaspoon dried rosemary
1 teaspoon dried thyme

1 teaspoon dried basil

½ teaspoon ground ginger

1 teaspoon juniper berries, crushed

6 black peppercorns

300 ml (½ pint) water

1.5 kg (3 lb) lean beef, rolled and tied

25 g (1 oz) butter

1 onion, chopped

1 carrot, chopped

1 celery stick

50 g (2 oz) mixed dried fruit

4 ginger snap biscuits

150 ml (5 fl oz) soured cream

salt

Put the red wine, wine vinegar, herbs, spices and water into a pan. Bring to the boil and then remove from the heat and allow to cool.

Put the beef into a china or glass bowl and pour over the red wine marinade. Cover and marinate for 3–5 days in the refrigerator, turning the meat at least once a day.

Remove the meat from the marinade and pat dry with kitchen paper. Reserve the marinade. Melt the butter in a large flameproof casserole, add the meat and brown it on all sides. Add the onion, carrot, celery and mixed fruit. Strain in the reserved marinade. Bring the liquid to the boil and cover the casserole with foil and a lid.

Put into a preheated oven, 150°C (300°F), Gas Mark 2, and cook for 3–4 hours until the beef is tender, turning the meat from time to time. When the meat is cooked, take it out of the casserole, cut into slices and arrange it on a serving dish. Keep the meat warm.

Skim any fat from the top of the liquid in the casserole, then pour the liquid, vegetables and dried fruit into a blender or food processor, add the ginger snaps and blend until smooth. Pour back into the casserole, add the soured cream, and reheat gently without boiling. Taste and adjust the seasoning, if necessary, and pour over the beef.

Serves 4–6

Montego Pepperpot

2 tablespoons oil

500 g (1 lb) shin of beef, diced

1 large onion, chopped

1 green chilli, deseeded and chopped

2 tomatoes, skinned, deseeded and diced

1 teaspoon dried thyme

300 ml (½ pint) beef stock

1–2 teaspoons Tabasco sauce

500 g (1 lb) yams, diced

500 g (1 lb) can red kidney beans, drained

salt and pepper

Heat the oil in a pan, add the beef and brown it on all sides. Transfer the beef to a casserole with a slotted spoon. Add the onion and chilli to the pan and cook until soft. Add the tomatoes, thyme, stock and Tabasco sauce to the pan. Season with salt and pepper and bring to the boil. Add the yams to the casserole, pour the stock over and mix well.

Cover the casserole, put into a preheated oven, 160°C (325°F), Gas Mark 3, and cook for 1½ hours. Add the kidney beans to the casserole and cook for a further 30 minutes. Serve immediately.

Serves 4

above: Montego pepperpot
left: Argentine beef peaches

Armenian Lamb

2 tablespoons olive oil

1 kg (2 lb) leg of lamb, tied

1 onion, chopped

175 g (6 oz) dried apricots

1 teaspoon ground coriander

1 teaspoon ground cumin

1 teaspoon ground cinnamon

900 ml(1½ pints) lamb stock

salt and pepper

To garnish:

25 g (1 oz) toasted pine nuts

apricot halves

sprig of rosemary

Heat the oil in a large flameproof casserole, brown the lamb on all sides, then add the onion to the pan and cook until it has softened slightly. Add the apricots and spices. Season with salt and pepper and add enough stock to come halfway up the lamb.

Bring to the boil, then cover the casserole and transfer to a preheated oven, 160°C (325°F), Gas Mark 3. Cook for 2 hours, turning the lamb from time to time. Remove the casserole from the oven. Remove the strings from the lamb and keep it warm in a deep serving dish.

Put the onion and apricots into a blender with enough stock from the casserole (fat skimmed off) to make 600 ml (1 pint). Blend to a smooth sauce and pour over the lamb. Garnish with pine nuts, apricot halves and rosemary.

Serves 4–6

Greek Lamb and Feta Cheese Casserole

750 g (1½ lb) boned weight leg of
   lamb, boned removed

3 tablespoons olive oil

1 large onion, finely chopped

1 garlic clove, crushed

425 g (14 oz) can tomatoes, drained
   and chopped

1 teaspoon dried oregano

125 g (4 oz) black olives, pitted and
   chopped

250 g (8 oz) feta cheese

salt and pepper

Cut the leg of lamb into thin slices. Heat the oil in a frying pan and fry the lamb slices a few at a time. Drain on kitchen paper.

Add the onions and garlic to the pan and cook for 2–3 minutes. Add the tomatoes, oregano and olives and season with salt and pepper.

Layer the meat and tomato mixture in a casserole, finishing with a layer of the tomato mixture. Crumble the feta cheese over the top. Cover the casserole, put into a preheated oven, 180°C (350°F), Gas Mark 4, and cook for 1½ hours.

Uncover and then place under a preheated hot grill to brown the cheese. Serve immediately.

Serves 4–6

Put 2 teaspoons of the lamb mixture into the centre of each vine leaf, using 2 leaves together if they are small, and fold the leaves up to make small packets. There should be about 24 packets in all.

Arrange the packets in a single layer, seam-side down, in a shallow casserole. Mix together the rest of the tomato purée and the water, the lemon juice and sugar and pour over the vine leaves.

Cover the casserole and cook in a preheated oven, 180°C (350°F), Gas Mark 4, for about 40 minutes.

Serves 4

Dolmades

1 tablespoon olive oil

1 onion, finely chopped

375 g (12 oz) minced lamb

2 tablespoons tomato purée

450 ml (¾ pint) water

175 g (6 oz) cooked long-grain rice

2 tablespoons parsley, chopped

250 g (8 oz) packet vine leaves

2 teaspoons lemon juice

½ teaspoon caster sugar

salt and pepper

Heat the oil in a pan, add the onion and lamb and cook until the lamb is no longer pink. Add 1 tablespoon of the tomato purée, 150 ml (¼ pint) of the water and season with salt and pepper. Bring to the boil, cover the pan and cook for about 20 minutes.

Remove the pan from the heat, add the rice and parsley to the pan and then mix well.

Put the vine leaves in a saucepan of boiling water and then cook for 5 minutes. Drain well.

far left: Greek lamb and feta cheese casserole
above: Armenian lamb
below: dolmades

Jambalaya

3 tablespoons oil

1 large onion, sliced

1 large green pepper, cored,
    deseeded and sliced

1 large red pepper, cored, deseeded
    and sliced

1 garlic clove, crushed

250 g (8 oz) long-grain rice

600 ml (1 pint) hot chicken stock

250 g (8 oz) piece cooked ham,
    diced

4 tomatoes, skinned, deseeded and
    cut into strips

225 g (8 oz) peeled cooked prawns

salt and pepper

To garnish:

8 whole prawns

sprigs of parsley

Heat the oil in a large flameproof casserole, add the onion, peppers and garlic and cook for 2–3 minutes. Add the rice to the pan and stir around until all the grains are coated with the oil. Pour in the stock and add the ham. Season with salt and pepper.

Bring to the boil, then cover the casserole with foil and a lid. Cook in a preheated oven, 190°C (375°F), Gas Mark 5, for 45 minutes.

Remove the casserole from the oven. There should be just a little liquid left – if not, you could add 2 or 3 tablespoons of stock. Add the tomatoes and prawns, then cover the casserole, return to the oven and cook for 10–15 minutes until the prawns and tomatoes are heated through and all the liquid has been absorbed. Serve immediately, garnished with the whole prawns and sprigs of parsley.

Serves 4

Calypso Pork

If guava jelly is not available, any clear yellow fruit jelly would make an acceptable substitute in this recipe.

2 tablespoons oil

1 onion, sliced

1 garlic clove, crushed

4 pork chops, about 250 g (8 oz)
    each, rind removed

2 tablespoons rum

1 teaspoon ground ginger

3 tablespoons guava jelly

1 tablespoon cornflour

75 ml (3 fl oz) water

salt and pepper

1 guava, peeled and sliced, to garnish

Heat the oil in a frying pan, add the onion and garlic and cook until soft, then transfer to a casserole.

Put the pork chops into the frying pan and cook for 2 minutes on each side. Pour the rum into the pan and ignite. When the flames have subsided, transfer the chops to the casserole.

Add the ginger and guava jelly to the pan and stir gently until the jelly has completely melted.

Mix the cornflour with the water, pour into the pan and bring to the boil, stirring. Season to taste with salt and pepper and then pour over the pork chops.

above: jambalaya
right: puchero

Cover the casserole and cook in a preheated oven, 190°C (375°F), Gas Mark 5, for 45 minutes. Serve garnished with the sliced guava.

Serves 4

Pork Avgolemono

2 tablespoons oil
1 large onion, chopped
500 g (1 lb) lean pork, diced
25 g (1 oz) plain flour
150 ml (¼ pint) dry white wine
300 ml (½ pint) light stock
500 g (1 lb) celeriac, diced
2 egg yolks
2 tablespoons lemon juice
1 tablespoon parsley, chopped
salt and pepper

Heat the oil in a large flameproof casserole. Add the onion and pork and fry gently for 2–3 minutes. Stir the flour into the casserole, cook for 1 minute and then add the wine, stock, celeriac and season with salt and pepper.

Bring to the boil, then cover the casserole and place in a preheated oven, 180°C (350°F), Gas Mark 4. Cook for 1–1½ hours until the pork is tender.

Remove the casserole from the oven and put back on the heat. Mix the egg yolks, lemon juice and parsley and stir in 3 tablespoons of stock from the casserole. Pour the sauce back into the casserole, stir and reheat gently but do not boil.

Serves 4

Puchero

2 tablespoons oil
1 onion, chopped
1 garlic clove, crushed
250 g (8 oz) carrots, diced
425 g (14 oz) can tomatoes
1 tablespoon wine vinegar
150 ml (¼ pint) water
1 bay leaf
½ teaspoon crushed dried red chillies
500 g (1 lb) piece salt pork, boned, rinded and soaked overnight
175 g (6 oz) chorizo sausage
500 g (1 lb) can red kidney beans, drained
sprigs of rosemary, to garnish

Heat the oil in a pan, then add the onion, garlic and carrots and cook for 2–3 minutes. Add the tomatoes and juice to the pan, then add the vinegar, water, bay leaf and crushed chillies. Bring to the boil.

Put the salt pork into a casserole. Pour the sauce over, then cover and cook in a preheated oven, 180°C (350°F), Gas Mark 4, for 2 hours. Add the chorizo sausage and beans to the casserole and cook for a further 30 minutes.

To serve, remove the pork and sausage from the casserole, slice them and arrange on a warmed serving dish. Remove the bay leaf and pour the sauce over the meats, garnishing the dish with some sprigs of rosemary.

Serves 4

Baccala

If salt cod is unavailable, you can use 500 g (1 lb) fresh cod. Omit the initial soaking, then proceed with the recipe.

500 g (1 lb) salt cod
2 tablespoons olive oil
1 onion, chopped
1 green pepper, cored, deseeded and chopped
1 garlic clove, crushed
425 g (14 oz) can chopped tomatoes, juice reserved
2 tablespoons parsley, chopped
500 g (1 lb) cooked potatoes, sliced
salt and pepper

Soak the salt cod in plenty of cold water for 24 hours, changing the water 3 or 4 times. Drain the fish and put into a saucepan of fresh cold water. Bring to the boil, then simmer for 15–20 minutes until the fish flakes easily. Drain and then leave until cold enough to handle. Skin, bone and flake the fish.

Heat the oil in a pan, add the onion, green pepper and garlic and cook gently for 2 minutes. Add the tomatoes and their juice and parsley, and season with salt and pepper. Bring to the boil and add the fish.

Layer the potatoes and fish mixture in a casserole, starting with the potatoes and ending with the fish. Cover the casserole, put into a preheated oven, 180°C (350°F), Gas Mark 4, and cook for 1 hour. Serve hot, garnished with wedges of hard-boiled egg.

Serves 4

left: baccala
above: *Chinese crab and rice casserole*
right: *prawns and okra in coconut sauce*

Chinese Crab and Rice Casserole

1 tablespoon oil

1 onion, chopped

2 celery sticks, sliced

375 g (12 oz) cooked long-grain rice

50 g (2 oz) frozen peas, thawed

250 g (8 oz) can water chestnuts, drained

250 g (8 oz) crabmeat

25 g (1 oz) butter

50 g (2 oz) blanched almonds

150 ml (¼ pint) tomato juice

1 tablespoon light soy sauce

salt and pepper

Heat the oil in a pan, add the onion and celery and cook until soft. Add to the rice in a mixing bowl with the thawed peas, water chestnuts and crabmeat.

Melt the butter in a pan and fry the almonds until lightly browned. Stir the almonds, tomato juice and soy sauce into the rice mixture. Season with salt and pepper and mix well.

Put the mixture into a casserole. Cover and cook in a preheated oven, 180°C (350°F), Gas Mark 4, for 25 minutes. Serve hot.

Serves 3–4

Prawns and Okra in Coconut Sauce

2 tablespoons oil

1 small onion, finely chopped

1 small green pepper, cored, deseeded and finely chopped

500 g (1 lb) small okra, stalk end removed

50 g (2 oz) creamed coconut

300 ml (½ pint) boiling water

1 tablespoon chilli sauce

1 tablespoon tomato purée

250 g (8 oz) peeled cooked prawns

salt and pepper

Heat the oil in a flameproof casserole, add the onion and green pepper and cook until soft. Add the okra to the casserole and cook for a further minute.

Dissolve the creamed coconut in the boiling water, and then add the chilli sauce and tomato purée. Season with salt and pepper, then pour the coconut mixture into the casserole and bring to the boil. Remove from the heat.

Cover the casserole and put into a preheated oven, 180°C (350°), Gas Mark 4, and cook for 30 minutes. Add the prawns to the casserole, mixing them in well. Cook the casserole, covered, for a further 10 minutes.

Serves 4

Vegetarian Warmers

Okra and Pasta Niçoise

2 tablespoons oil

1 onion, chopped

1 garlic clove, crushed

425 g (14 oz) can chopped tomatoes

300 ml (½ pint) vegetable stock

500 g (1 lb) okra, stalk end removed and halved

1 teaspoon dried marjoram

375 g (12 oz) pasta bows

50 g (2 oz) black olives, pitted

salt and pepper

Heat the oil in a large flameproof casserole, add the onion and garlic and cook for 2–3 minutes. Add the tomatoes and their juice, stock, okra and marjoram. Season with salt and pepper and bring to the boil. Cover the casserole and then cook in a preheated oven, 180°C (350°F), Gas Mark 4, for 40 minutes.

While the okra is cooking, add the pasta to a pan of boiling salted water and cook for about 8-10 minutes, or according to the packet instructions, until *al dente*. Drain well and rinse with cold water.

After 40 minutes, add the pasta and olives to the casserole and mix well. Cover the casserole again and cook for a further 15 minutes.

Serves 4

Italian Bean Casserole

125 g (4 oz) red kidney beans, soaked overnight

125 g (4 oz) cannellini beans, soaked overnight

125 g (4 oz) flageolet beans, soaked overnight

2 tablespoons olive oil

1 onion, chopped

1 green pepper, cored, deseeded and chopped

1 teaspoon dried oregano

150 g (5 oz) can tomato purée

300 ml (½ pint) water

1 teaspoon caster sugar

salt and pepper

sprig of oregano, to garnish

Cook the beans separately to avoid the red beans colouring the others.

Cover with cold water and bring to the boil. Boil rapidly for 10 minutes. Reduce the heat and simmer until the beans are just cooked.

Heat the oil in a pan, add the onion and green pepper and cook until soft. Add the oregano, tomato purée, water, sugar, salt and pepper and bring to the boil.

Drain the beans, put into a large casserole and pour the onion and pepper sauce over them. Cook in a preheated oven, 160°C (325°F), Gas Mark 3, uncovered, for 1 hour, stirring occasionally, until most of the liquid has been absorbed. Serve the casserole garnished with sprigs of oregano.

Serves 4

Mixed Bean Casserole with Cashew Crumble

Cashews are very high in protein but any other chopped nuts may be used. Breadcrumbs and wheatgerm can be substituted for the rolled oats or, if nuts are not used, add grated cheese to the crumble mixture for extra protein.

250 g (8 oz) shelled weight broad
    beans
250 g (8 oz) runner beans, trimmed
    and sliced
125 g (4 oz) French beans, topped
    and tailed

25 g (1 oz) butter
25 g (1 oz) plain flour
300 ml (½ pint) milk
2 tablespoons parsley, chopped
salt and pepper
Topping:
75 g (3 oz) butter
125 g (4 oz) plain flour
50 g (2 oz) rolled oats
50 g (2 oz) salted cashew nuts,
    chopped

Put the broad beans into a pan of boiling salted water and cook for 5 minutes, then add the runner beans and French beans and cook for a further 5 minutes. Drain the beans well, and then place in a shallow casserole.

Melt the butter in a clean pan, add the flour and cook, stirring, for 2 minutes. Add the milk and bring to the boil, stirring all the time,

then simmer for 2–3 minutes. Add the parsley and season to taste with salt and pepper, then pour over the beans and mix well.

Rub the butter into the flour with the fingertips, then add the rolled oats and cashew nuts and stir well.

Sprinkle the crumble topping over the beans, pressing it down lightly. Place the casserole in a preheated oven, 200°C (400°F), Gas Mark 6, and cook for 40 minutes. Serve hot with steamed vegetables or a crisp winter salad.

Serves 4

left: okra and pasta Niçoise
below: Italian bean casserole

Boston Baked Beans

375 g (12 oz) haricot beans, soaked
  overnight
3 tablespoons oil
1 onion, chopped
1 garlic clove, crushed
1 tablespoon wholegrain mustard
1 tablespoon molasses or black
  treacle
150 g (5 oz) can tomato purée
1 tablespoon soft brown sugar
salt and pepper
tomato slices and parsley, to garnish

Put the beans in a saucepan and cover with cold water. Bring to the boil and boil rapidly for 10 minutes. Reduce the heat and then simmer for a further 30 minutes. Drain the beans, reserving 600 ml (1 pint) of the cooking liquid.

Heat the oil in a pan, add the onion and garlic and cook gently until softened and lightly browned.

Put the beans into a casserole, add the onion and garlic and any remaining oil. Add the mustard, molasses or treacle, tomato purée and sugar. Season with salt and pepper, then mix in the reserved cooking liquid.

Cover the casserole with foil and a lid, place in a preheated oven, 140°C (275°F), Gas Mark 1, and cook for 4 hours, stirring gently from time to time.

Serves 4

Mexican Bean Stew

2 tablespoons oil
2 onions, chopped
1 garlic clove, crushed
2 red chillies, deseeded and chopped
625 g (1¼ lb) pumpkin
2 fresh corn cobs
2 x 425 g (14 oz) cans chopped
  tomatoes
2 x 425 g (14 oz) cans haricot beans
salt and pepper
2 tablespoons fresh coriander,
  chopped, to garnish
To serve:
soured cream
diced avocado

Heat the oil and fry the onions and garlic until soft and golden. Add the chillies and cook for 2–3 minutes.

Remove the rind and seeds from the pumpkin and cut the flesh into large chunks. With a knife, remove the kernels from the corn cobs.

Add the pumpkin and corn to the pan with the tomatoes and drained beans. Simmer gently for 20–30 minutes. If the consistency is too thick, add a little vegetable stock to thin the sauce. Season to taste with salt and pepper.

Serve hot, garnished with a sprinkling of fresh coriander. Top each serving with a spoonful of soured cream and some diced avocado. Plain boiled rice or warm flour tortillas make a good accompaniment.

Serves 4

Black-eye Bean Stroganoff

375 g (12 oz) black-eye beans, soaked
  overnight
2 tablespoons oil
1 large onion, sliced
1 garlic clove, crushed
375 g (12 oz) mushrooms, sliced
2 teaspoons paprika
1 tablespoon tomato purée
150 ml (¼ pint) vegetable stock
150 ml (¼ pint) soured cream
salt and pepper
paprika, to garnish

Put the black-eye beans into a large saucepan of cold water, bring to the boil and boil rapidly for 10 minutes. Reduce the heat and then simmer gently for 20–30 minutes. The beans should be tender and cooked but still firm. Do not overcook them or they will be mushy.

While the beans are cooking, heat the oil in a large frying pan, and then fry the onion, garlic and mushrooms for about 2–3 minutes, stirring occasionally, until softened and golden. Add the paprika to the pan and cook for a further minute.

Drain the black-eye beans and transfer to a casserole dish. Add the onion, garlic and mushrooms, the tomato purée and vegetable stock to the casserole. Season to taste with salt and pepper.

Stir well, then cover the casserole dish and place in a preheated oven, 180°C (350°F), Gas Mark 4, and cook for 40 minutes.

Remove the casserole from the oven, uncover and gently swirl in the soured cream. Sprinkle with a dusting of paprika and serve hot. A good accompaniment would be some boiled rice and a crisp salad.

Serves 4

left: Boston baked beans
below: black-eye bean stroganoff

Chickpea and Cauliflower Curry

175 g (6 oz) chickpeas, soaked
    overnight
3–4 tablespoons oil
1 onion, chopped
1 garlic clove, crushed
175 g (6 oz) carrots, diced
250 g (8 oz) cauliflower florets
2 teaspoons ground turmeric
1 teaspoon ground cinnamon
½ teaspoon ground coriander
½ teaspoon ground ginger
½ teaspoon garam masala
½ teaspoon chilli powder
1 large potato, diced
salt and pepper
parsley, to garnish

Put the chickpeas in a saucepan,
and then cover with cold water and
bring to the boil. Boil rapidly for
10 minutes, then reduce the heat
and cook for 30–40 minutes until
tender. Drain the chickpeas and
transfer to a casserole dish. Reserve
the cooking liquid.

Heat the oil in a pan, add the
onion and garlic and cook until
soft, then transfer to the casserole.
Add the carrots and cauliflower
to the pan, cook until lightly
browned and transfer them to
the casserole.

Put all the spices into the pan,
adding a little extra oil if necessary.
Cook gently for 1 minute, and then
add some of the reserved liquid,
potato and season with salt and
pepper. Bring to the boil and pour
into the casserole. Cover and cook
in a preheated oven, 180°C (350°F),
Gas Mark 4, for 1–1¼ hours, stirring
from time to time.

Serves 3–4

Aubergines Stuffed with Pine Nuts

2 large aubergines, about
    375 g (12 oz) each
25 g (1 oz) butter
1 large onion, chopped
1 garlic clove, crushed
50 g (2 oz) pine nuts
4 large tomatoes, skinned, deseeded
    and chopped
1 tablespoon tomato purée
1 teaspoon dried oregano
2 teaspoons paprika
4–5 tablespoons olive oil

150 ml (¼ pint) vegetable stock
salt and pepper

First, remove the stalks from the aubergines and cut each one in half lengthways. Cut each half into three slices lengthways. Put the slices in a colander, sprinkle with some salt and leave for 30 minutes to drain.

While the aubergines are draining, make the filling. Melt the butter in a pan, add the onion and garlic and cook until soft. Add the pine nuts and stir until lightly browned. Add the tomatoes, tomato purée, oregano and paprika to the pan. Season with pepper. Stir well and cook gently to a thick purée.

Rinse the aubergine slices in cold water and dry on kitchen paper. Heat the oil in a frying pan and fry the aubergine slices, a few at a time, for about 1 minute each side. Remove and drain on kitchen paper.

Reassemble the aubergine halves by spreading about 1 tablespoon of the filling between each slice and pressing the slices together. Put the aubergine halves into a shallow casserole dish and pour over the stock. Cover the casserole and cook in a preheated oven, 180°C (350°F), Gas Mark 4, for 45–50 minutes.

Serves 2

above left: chickpea and cauliflower curry
below left: aubergines stuffed with pine nuts
right: spiced red cabbage and beetroot casserole with chestnuts

Spiced Red Cabbage and Beetroot Casserole with Chestnuts

50 g (2 oz) butter
1 large onion, sliced
500 g (1 lb) red cabbage, shredded
250 g (8 oz) cooking apple, peeled, cored and chopped
375 g (12 oz) peeled chestnuts or 300 g (10 oz) canned whole chestnuts
2 tablespoons soft brown sugar
1 tablespoon red wine vinegar
½ teaspoon ground nutmeg
½ teaspoon ground cinnamon
300 ml (½ pint) water
250 g (8 oz) cooked beetroot, diced
salt and pepper
apple slices and parsley, to garnish

Melt the butter in a flameproof casserole, add the onion and cook until soft. Add the red cabbage and apple and stir well together until the cabbage is well coated with the melted butter.

Add the chestnuts, brown sugar, vinegar, spices and water to the casserole. Season with salt and pepper and stir well. Bring to the boil, cover and cook in a preheated oven, 180°C (350°F), Gas Mark 4, for 1 hour until the chestnuts are cooked. Add the beetroot to the casserole and then cook in the oven for a further 5 minutes. Serve hot.

Serves 4

Mushroom and Raisin Pilaff

The final 5–10 minutes' cooking of the rice takes place in the heat left in the pan after it has been removed from the oven. In this way, the grains remain separate and the texture of the rice retains a slight bite.

25 g (1 oz) butter
1 tablespoon oil
1 large onion, finely chopped
1 garlic clove, crushed
250 g (8 oz) brown rice, washed and well drained
125 g (4 oz) button mushrooms, thinly sliced
½ teaspoon dried dill
½ teaspoon turmeric
450 ml (¾ pint) vegetable stock
50 g (2 oz) seedless raisins
salt and pepper
To garnish:
broccoli spears

Heat the butter and oil in a shallow, flameproof casserole and gently fry the onion and garlic for 3–4 minutes until tender and lightly browned. Add the rice, mushrooms, dill and turmeric and continue cooking for 1–2 minutes, stirring all the time. Pour in the vegetable stock and, if necessary, season lightly with salt and pepper.

Cover closely with a lid or foil and then cook in a preheated oven, 180°C (350°F), Gas Mark 4, for about 35 minutes. Stir in the raisins, cover the casserole and return to the oven for 10 minutes or until all the stock has been absorbed.

Leave the lid on and stand the casserole in a warm place for about 5–10 minutes to complete the cooking, then transfer the pilaff to a hot serving dish, using a fork to keep the grains separate. Garnish with tomatoes and broccoli.

Serves 4

Neapolitan Pasta Casserole

175 g (6 oz) wholewheat pasta spirals
50 g (2 oz) butter
1 large onion, finely chopped
1 garlic clove, crushed (optional)
3 tablespoons tomato purée
1 teaspoon dried oregano or basil
150 ml (¼ pint) wine
500 g (1 lb) courgettes, thinly sliced
25 g (1 oz) Parmesan cheese, finely grated
salt and pepper

Cook the pasta in a pan of boiling salted water for 12-14 minutes or according to packet instructions. Drain well.

Meanwhile, heat the butter in a pan and fry the onion and garlic, if using, for 4–5 minutes until tender and lightly browned. Blend in the tomato purée and oregano or basil, then stir in the wine. Season well with salt and pepper.

Arrange alternate layers of cooked pasta and courgettes in a buttered casserole, finishing with a layer of courgettes, then spoon the onion and wine mixture over the top.

Cover with a lid or foil and cook in a preheated oven, 200°C (400°F), Gas Mark 6, for 30 minutes. Remove

the cover, sprinkle the top with Parmesan and return to the oven for 20 minutes or until the top is golden brown and crisp and the courgettes are tender.

Serves 4

Vegetarian Hot Pot

175 g (6 oz) lentils

50 g (2 oz) butter

250 g (8 oz) carrots, very thinly sliced

250 g (8 oz) potatoes, very thinly
  sliced

375 g (12 oz) leeks, trimmed and
  sliced

125 g (4 oz) mushrooms, thinly
  sliced

3–4 tablespoons parsley, finely
  chopped

1 tablespoon tomato purée

150 ml (¼ pint) red wine

150 ml (¼ pint) vegetable stock

salt and pepper

To garnish:

sliced mushrooms

sprigs of parsley

Nut topping:

125 g (4 oz) butter, softened

50 g (2 oz) wholemeal flour

50 g (2 oz) jumbo oats

125 g (4 oz) mixed nuts, chopped

50 g (2 oz) Cheddar cheese, finely
  grated

Place the lentils in a pan, cover with water and season with salt. Bring to

the boil and simmer for 45 minutes or until tender. Drain well.

Meanwhile, heat the butter in a large saucepan, add the carrots, potatoes and leeks and fry gently for 10 minutes until lightly browned, stirring occasionally.

Arrange layers of the fried vegetables, mushrooms and lentils in a well-greased deep casserole, sprinkling each layer lightly with salt, pepper and chopped parsley, and reserving a few mushrooms for the garnish. Blend the tomato purée, wine and stock and add to the casserole.

Cover closely with a lid or foil and cook in a preheated oven, 180°C (350°F), Gas Mark 4, for about 1 hour or until the vegetables are cooked and tender.

To make the nut topping, blend together the butter, flour, oats, nuts and cheese and season with salt and pepper. Remove the casserole from the oven, spoon the nut topping over the top so that the surface is covered completely, and return to the oven for 30 minutes or until the top is crisp and golden. Garnish with mushrooms and parsley sprigs.

Serves 4

Variation:

Dubarry Hotpot Omit the potatoes and add ¼ cauliflower, broken into florets, at the same time as the carrots and leeks.

left: mushroom and raisin pilaff
above: vegetarian hot pot

Vegetable Dhansak

125 g (4 oz) red lentils
2 tablespoons oil
1 onion, chopped
1 garlic clove, crushed
1 teaspoon ground cumin
½ teaspoon ground coriander
1 teaspoon cardamom seeds
pinch of ground cinnamon
2 teaspoons white wine vinegar
1 tablespoon mild lime pickle
450 ml (¾ pint) water
250 g (8 oz) aubergine, stalk removed
    and diced
250 g (8 oz) sweet potato, diced
250 g (8 oz) potato, diced
salt and pepper
sprig of fresh coriander, to garnish

Put the lentils into a pan of cold water, bring to the boil and simmer for 10 minutes. Drain well.

Heat the oil in a pan, add the onion and garlic and cook until soft. Add all the spices and cook for 1 minute. Add the vinegar, pickle and water and bring to the boil.

Put the lentils into a casserole, add the contents of the pan, the aubergine, sweet potato and potato. Season with salt and pepper and mix well. Cover and cook in a preheated oven, 160°C (325°F), Gas Mark 3, for 1 hour, stirring gently from time to time. Serve garnished with fresh coriander.

Serves 4

Sag Dhal

2 tablespoons oil
1 onion, chopped
1 garlic clove, crushed
1 teaspoon fresh root ginger, grated
½ teaspoon ground turmeric
1 teaspoon ground cumin
1 teaspoon mustard seeds
½ teaspoon cayenne pepper
175 g (6 oz) whole green lentils,
    soaked overnight
600 ml (1 pint) water
500 g (1 lb) spinach, washed and
    shredded, or 250 g (8 oz) frozen
    leaf spinach, thawed
salt
150 ml (5 fl oz) natural yogurt, to
    serve

Heat the oil in a large flameproof casserole, add the onion, garlic and ginger and cook for 2 minutes, then add the turmeric, cumin, mustard seeds and cayenne and cook for a further minute.

Add the drained lentils to the casserole with the water and bring to the boil, and then add the spinach and salt to taste.

Cover the casserole, put into a preheated oven, 160°C (325°F), Gas Mark 3, and cook for about 1 hour, stirring gently from time to time. Spoon the yogurt over the casserole before serving.

Serves 4

Mushroom and Millet Casserole with Coriander

250 g (8 oz) millet

50 g (2 oz) butter

1 onion, chopped

2 garlic cloves, cubed

500 g (1 lb) flat mushrooms, diced

2 teaspoons soy sauce

75 ml (3 fl oz) water

1 teaspoon ground coriander

2 tablespoons fresh coriander, chopped

3–4 tomatoes, skinned and sliced

salt and pepper

Put the millet into a pan of lightly salted water, bring to the boil and then reduce the heat and simmer for about 30 minutes until tender.

Melt the butter in a pan, add the onion and garlic and cook gently for 2 minutes. Add the mushrooms and cook for a further 3 minutes, turning the mushrooms in the butter until golden brown.

Drain the cooked millet in a colander, then combine the millet and mushroom mixture in a casserole dish. Add the soy sauce, water, and ground and fresh coriander. Stir the mixture well, then taste and season with salt and pepper, if necessary.

Cover the casserole and cook in a preheated oven, 180°C (350°F), Gas Mark 4, for 30 minutes.

Remove the casserole from the oven, uncover and arrange the sliced tomatoes on top of the millet. Return to the oven, uncovered, and cook for a further 10 minutes. Serve immediately.

Serves 4

above left: sag dhal
above: vegetable dhansak
left: mushroom and millet casserole with coriander

Desserts

water. Check regularly and top up the water as and when necessary. Be careful not to let it boil dry.

To make the chocolate sauce, melt the chocolate with the syrup and water in a small bowl set over a saucepan of boiling water, and then beat until smooth.

Turn the pudding out onto a warmed serving dish and pour the hot sauce over before serving.

Serves 4

Chocolate Pudding

175 g (6 oz) self-raising flour

2 tablespoons cocoa powder

125 g (4 oz) butter or margarine

125 g (4 oz) caster sugar

2 large eggs

2 tablespoons milk

Chocolate sauce:

75 g (3 oz) plain chocolate, broken into pieces

3 tablespoons golden syrup

2 tablespoons water

Butter a 1.2 litre (2 pint) pudding basin. Sift the flour and cocoa together. Cream the fat and sugar together until light and fluffy. Beat in the eggs, one at a time, adding a little of the flour and cocoa with the second egg. Fold in the remaining flour and cocoa with a metal spoon and then mix in the milk.

Spoon the mixture into the buttered pudding basin. Cover with buttered foil, making a pleat across the centre to allow the pudding to rise. Steam for 1½–2 hours in the top of a steamer or by standing the basin in a covered pan of simmering

Eve's Pudding

500 g (1 lb) cooking apples, peeled, cored and thinly sliced

50 g (2 oz) soft brown sugar

125 g (4 oz) butter or margarine

125 g (4 oz) caster sugar

2 eggs

125 g (4 oz) self-raising flour, sifted

1 tablespoon hot water

Put the apples in a greased 1.2 litre (2 pint) shallow ovenproof dish and sprinkle with the brown sugar.

Cream the butter or margarine with the caster sugar until light and fluffy. Add the eggs, one at a time, adding a little flour with the second egg. Fold in the remaining flour, then the hot water.

Spread the mixture evenly over the apples and bake in a preheated

oven, 180°C (350°F), Gas Mark 4 for 40–45 minutes until golden brown. Serve hot with cream or custard.

Serves 4

Brown Betty

10 slices white bread, crusts removed

75 g (3 oz) butter

750 g–1 kg (1½–2 lb) cooking apples, peeled, cored and sliced

75 g (3 oz) soft brown sugar

Spread the bread thickly with butter and cut each slice into 4. Butter a 1.5 litre (2½ pint) ovenproof dish generously and line with some of the bread, butter-side down.

Cover with half of the apples, sprinkle with sugar and arrange another layer of bread over the top. Cover with the remaining apples, sprinkle with sugar and top with the remaining bread, butter-side up and slightly overlapping. Sprinkle with the remaining sugar.

Cover with foil and then bake in a preheated oven, 180°C (350°F),

Gas Mark 4, for 35 minutes. Remove the foil and then bake for a further 5 minutes until crisp and golden. Serve hot with custard or cream.

Serves 6

left: Eve's pudding
above: brown Betty

Lemon Pudding

50 g (2 oz) butter or margarine
grated rind and juice of 1 large lemon
75 g (3 oz) caster sugar
2 eggs, separated
25 g (1 oz) plain flour, sifted
175 ml (6 fl oz) milk

Grease a 600 ml (1 pint) ovenproof dish. Cream the butter or margarine with the lemon rind and sugar until light and fluffy.

Mix in the egg yolks, flour and lemon juice, then gradually stir in the milk. In a clean dry bowl, whisk the egg whites until stiff and then fold gently with a metal spoon in a figure-of-eight motion into the lemon mixture.

Turn the mixture into the greased ovenproof dish and then stand in a roasting pan, containing about 2.5 cm (1 inch) water. Bake the pudding in a preheated oven, 180°C (350°F), Gas Mark 4, for 40–45 minutes. Serve hot. The top will have cooked to an appetizing lemon sponge with a delicious lemon custard underneath. Serve with cream or crème fraîche.

Serves 4

above: lemon pudding, blackberry and apple crumble

Blackberry and Apple Crumble

75 g (3 oz) butter

175 g (6 oz) wholemeal flour

75 g (3 oz) demerara sugar

500 g (1 lb) cooking apples, peeled, cored and sliced

250 g (8 oz) blackberries

75 g (3 oz) sugar

Rub the butter into the flour until the mixture resembles breadcrumbs, and then stir in the demerara sugar. Layer the apples, blackberries and sugar in a buttered 900 ml (1½ pint) ovenproof dish. Sprinkle the crumble mixture over the fruit to cover completely.

Bake the fruit crumble in a preheated oven, 200°C (400°F), Gas Mark 6, for 40–50 minutes until golden brown. Serve hot or cold with cream or custard.

Serves 4–6

Variation:

Blackberry and Pear Crumble:
Substitute 500 g (1 lb) cooking pears for the cooking apples. Make as in the recipe above but bake in a preheated oven, 200°C (400°F), Gas Mark 6, for 15 minutes, then reduce the heat to 190°C (375°F), Gas Mark 5, and bake for a further 20–25 minutes.

Tarte Tatin

1.5 kg (3 lb) crisp dessert apples, e.g. Granny Smiths

75 g (3 oz) caster sugar

75 g (3 oz) butter

250 g (8 oz) puff pastry, thawed if frozen

Caramel:

75 g (3 oz) caster sugar

3 tablespoons water

25 g (1 oz) butter

Make the caramel. Put the sugar and water in a flameproof oval or round baking dish and place over a low heat. Stir until the sugar dissolves, then increase the heat and cook until the sugar starts to caramelize and go golden brown. Remove from the heat and stir in the butter.

Peel and core the apples, cut in half and pack tightly into the dish, arranging them in circles. Sprinkle with sugar and scatter the butter over the top. Cook in a preheated oven at 190°C (375°F), Gas Mark 5, for 20 minutes. Remove from the oven and increase the temperature to 220°C (425°F), Gas Mark 7.

Roll out the pastry and place on top of the apples. Tuck in the pastry edges round the sides of the dish.

Bake for a further 15–20 minutes until the pastry is crisp and golden, then cool and invert the tart onto a serving plate. Serve with cream.

Serves 4

Plum and Walnut Crumble

500 g (1 lb) plums, halved and stoned

75 g (3 oz) granulated sugar

175 g (6 oz) plain flour

75 g (3 oz) butter

75 g (3 oz) demerara sugar

125 g (4 oz) walnut pieces

Arrange the plums in a 1.2 litre (2 pint) ovenproof dish and sprinkle with the granulated sugar.

Sift the flour into a mixing bowl. Rub in the butter until it resembles fine breadcrumbs. Stir in the sugar and walnut pieces.

Spoon the crumble topping over the fruit. Bake in a preheated oven, 180°C (350°F), Gas Mark 4, for 30–40 minutes until golden.

Serves 4

Note: Try other combinations: cherry and almond or apple and mixed nuts.

mixture forms a soft, sticky topping which will run down the sides. Serve hot with cream.

Serves 6–8

Ginger Queen of Puddings

600 ml (1 pint) milk
pared rind of ½ lemon
50 g (2 oz) butter
175 g (6 oz) caster sugar
75 g (3 oz) fine fresh white
  breadcrumbs
3 eggs, separated
3–4 tablespoons ginger marmalade

Chocolate Fudge Pudding

2 eggs
125 g (4 oz) caster sugar
125 g (4 oz) butter or margarine
125 g (4 oz) self-raising flour
1 teaspoon baking powder
Fudge topping:
40 g (1½ oz) butter
40 g (1½ oz) soft dark brown sugar
40 g (1½ oz) golden syrup
15 g (½ oz) cocoa powder
2 tablespoons single or half cream
50 g (2 oz) walnuts or pecans, finely
  chopped

Grease and line a 20 cm (8 inch) sandwich tin or a 1.5 litre (2½ pint) ring mould. Place all the fudge ingredients in a small heavy-based saucepan. Heat gently until boiling, stirring constantly, and then boil for 30 seconds. Pour into the prepared tin or mould and leave until cold.

Place the eggs, sugar, fat, flour and baking powder in a large bowl and beat with a wooden spoon for 2 minutes. Turn out onto the cooled fudge mixture and spread evenly with a palette knife.

Bake in a preheated oven, 160°C (325°F), Gas Mark 3, for about 40–45 minutes, until the pudding is well risen, golden brown and firm to the touch. Leave in the tin or mould for 5 minutes before turning out the pudding.

Invert onto a serving plate and peel off the lining paper. The fudge

Butter a shallow 1.2 litre (2 pint) ovenproof dish. Put the milk and lemon rind in a saucepan set over a very low heat and leave for about 10 minutes. Discard the lemon rind.

Add the butter and 50 g (2 oz) of the sugar to the milk and stir until melted. Add the breadcrumbs and egg yolks and mix well. Transfer to the buttered ovenproof dish.

Leave to stand for 10 minutes, then bake in a preheated oven, 180°C (350°F), Gas Mark 4, for 15–20 minutes or until set. Cool slightly and then spread with the marmalade. Reduce the oven temperature to 150°C (300°F), Gas Mark 2.

Whisk the egg whites in a clean, dry bowl until stiff. Whisk in half of the remaining sugar, then fold in all but 2 teaspoons of the rest. Pipe or spoon the meringue over the baked pudding and sprinkle with the reserved sugar. Return to the cool oven for 8–10 minutes until golden.

Serves 6

Pineapple Pudding

425 g (14 oz) can pineapple slices, drained
15 g (½ oz) angelica
125 g (4 oz) butter or margarine
125 g (4 oz) caster sugar
grated rind and juice of 1 lemon
2 eggs
150 g (5 oz) self-raising flour, sifted

Butter a 900 ml (1½ pint) pudding basin and arrange the drained pineapple slices around the base and sides. Place a piece of angelica in the centre of each.

Cream the butter or margarine, sugar and lemon rind together until light and fluffy. Add the eggs, one at a time, adding a little flour with the second egg to prevent the mixture curdling. Beat thoroughly, and then fold in the remaining flour with the lemon juice.

Turn the mixture into the basin. Cover with buttered foil, making a pleat across the centre to allow the pudding to rise. Steam in the top of a steamer or by standing the basin in a covered pan of simmering water for 1½–2 hours. Top up the water as and when necessary. Do not allow it to boil dry.

Turn out the pudding onto a warmed serving dish and serve with cream or custard.

Serves 4

*above left: chocolate fudge pudding
left: ginger queen of puddings
above: pineapple pudding*

Apricot Upside-down Pudding

175 g (6 oz) butter or margarine
50 g (2 oz) soft brown sugar
425 g (14 oz) can apricot halves, or
  cooked fresh apricots, halved and
  pitted
125 g (4 oz) caster sugar
2 eggs
125 g (4 oz) self-raising flour, sifted
1 teaspoon ground mixed spice

Cream 50 g (2 oz) of the fat, mix with the brown sugar and spread over the bottom of a 1.2 litre (2 pint) ovenproof dish. Drain the apricots, reserving 1 tablespoon juice. Arrange in the dish.

Cream the remaining fat with the caster sugar until light and fluffy. Add the eggs, one at a time, adding a tablespoon of the flour with the last two. Beat thoroughly, then fold in the remaining flour, mixed spice and reserved apricot juice.

Spread over the apricots and bake in a preheated oven, 180°C (350°F), Gas Mark 4, for 55–60 minutes until the sponge springs back when it is lightly pressed with a finger.

Turn out onto a warmed serving dish and serve with cream.

Serves 6

Blackberry and Apple Layer

125 g (4 oz) butter
500 g (1 lb) cooking apples, peeled,
  cored and sliced
250 g (8 oz) blackberries
75 g (3 oz) demerara sugar
125 g (4 oz) fresh breadcrumbs

Melt 25 g (1 oz) of the butter in a pan. Add the apples, blackberries and 25 g (1 oz) of the sugar. Cover and simmer gently until soft but not pulpy.

Melt the remaining butter in a frying pan and fry the breadcrumbs until golden brown. Cool and then add the remaining sugar.

Divide half of the fruit between 4 individual glass dishes and cover with half of the crumbs, then repeat the layers. Serve well chilled with whipped cream.

Serves 4

Christmas Pudding

175 g (6 oz) plain flour
2 teaspoons ground mixed spice
1 teaspoon ground cinnamon
½ teaspoon grated nutmeg
175 g (6 oz) fresh white breadcrumbs
175 g (6 oz) butter
175 g (6 oz) soft brown sugar
375 g (12 oz) sultanas
250 g (8 oz) raisins
250 g (8 oz) currants
75 g (3 oz) chopped mixed peel
grated rind and juice of 1 orange
2 eggs, beaten
125 ml (4 fl oz) brown ale
sprig of holly, to decorate
To serve:
2-3 tablespoons brandy, optional
cream or brandy butter

Grease a 1.75 litre (3 pint) pudding basin. Sift the flour and spices into a bowl, add the breadcrumbs and rub in the butter with the fingertips. Stir in the sugar, add the remaining ingredients and mix thoroughly.

Turn into the greased pudding basin, cover with a pudding cloth or greaseproof paper and foil, and steam for 6 hours, topping up the pan with boiling water as necessary.

Cool slightly, then remove the cloth or paper and leave to cool completely. Cover with some clean greaseproof paper and foil and store in a cool dry place.

To serve, steam the pudding again for 2–2½ hours. Turn out onto a warmed serving dish. If liked, pour over 2–3 tablespoons warmed brandy and ignite. Top with a sprig of holly and serve with cream or brandy butter.

Serves 8–10

right: Christmas pudding, blackberry and apple layer

Bread and Butter Pudding

9 slices white bread, crusts
  removed

50 g (2 oz) butter

50 g (2 oz) sultanas or currants

50 g (2 oz) caster sugar

2 large eggs

600 ml (1 pint) milk

grated nutmeg

Butter a 1.2 litre (2 pint) ovenproof
dish. Spread the bread thickly with
butter and then cut each slice into
4. Arrange half in the buttered dish,
buttered-side down. Sprinkle with
the fruit and half of the sugar, and
then cover with the remaining
bread, butter-side up.

Beat the eggs and milk together
and strain over the top of the
pudding. Sprinkle with the
remaining sugar and nutmeg to
taste and leave for 30 minutes.

Bake the pudding in a preheated
oven, 160°C (325°F), Gas Mark 3,
for 50–60 minutes until the top is
golden brown and crisp. Serve hot
with custard or cream.

Serves 4

above: bread and butter pudding
right: apple and date pudding

Apple and Date Pudding

125 g (4 oz) self-raising flour
50 g (2 oz) fresh white breadcrumbs
pinch of salt
75 g (3 oz) shredded suet
25 g (1 oz) caster sugar
125 g (4 oz) apple, peeled and finely chopped
125 g (4 oz) dates, chopped
grated rind of 1 lemon
150 ml (¼ pint) milk (approximately)

Grease a 900 ml (1½ pint) pudding basin. Mix together the flour, breadcrumbs, salt, suet and sugar. Stir in the apple, dates and lemon rind. Make a well in the centre and add enough milk to give a soft dropping consistency.

Transfer to the greased pudding basin, cover with some greased foil, pleated down the centre, and then tie up with string.

Place the basin in a steamer or a large saucepan, which has been half-filled with boiling water. Cover and cook for 1½–2 hours, topping up the water as and when necessary.

Remove the foil and turn the pudding out onto a serving plate. Serve with custard.

Serves 6

Treacle Pudding

125 g (4 oz) butter or margarine
125 g (4 oz) caster sugar
2 large eggs
125 g (4 oz) self-raising flour, sifted
4 tablespoons golden syrup
Sauce:
4 tablespoons golden syrup
1 tablespoon water

Butter a 900 ml (1½ pint) pudding basin. Cream the butter or margarine and sugar together until light and fluffy. Beat in the eggs, one at a time, adding a little of the flour with the second egg. Fold in the remaining flour.

Spoon the golden syrup into the prepared pudding basin, then put the sponge mixture on top. Cover with buttered foil, making a pleat across the centre to allow the pudding to rise.

Steam for 1½–2 hours in the top of a steamer or by standing the basin in a covered pan of simmering water. Top up the water as and when necessary. Take care not to let it boil dry.

To make the sauce, heat the syrup and water in a small pan. Turn the pudding out onto a warmed serving dish and pour the hot sauce over before serving.

Serves 4

Index